THE PRICE OF POWER

THE CHICAGO HISTORY OF AMERICAN CIVILIZATION

Daniel J. Boorstin, EDITOR

The
Price of Power

America since 1945

By
Herbert Agar

THE UNIVERSITY OF CHICAGO PRESS

Library of Congress Catalog Number: 57-8575

THE UNIVERSITY OF CHICAGO PRESS, CHICAGO 37
The University of Toronto Press, Toronto 5, Canada

© *1957 by The University of Chicago. Published 1957*
Second Impression 1958. Composed and printed by THE
UNIVERSITY OF CHICAGO PRESS, *Chicago, Illinois, U.S.A.*

For Barbie

Editor's Preface

In the decade after 1945 the world no longer centered on Europe, and America's rise to dominance sharpened all the issues of American life and the American conscience. Mr. Agar describes in this book the bewilderment of Americans before their new role, but he is not himself bewildered. He tells us that the United States cannot fulfil its mission merely by providing an example to the world but must speak decisively in the council of nations. The question before the American people has been simply whether they would speak well or badly, for even their silence is momentously construed. Our spiritual unreadiness for this role and our refusal to face this question, according to Mr. Agar, explain much of our dissatisfaction with ourselves and our distrust of one another. Americans who see themselves in Mr. Agar's history will not find a flattering image; but, if his image is accurate, they dare not shut their eyes.

vii

Editor's Preface

The boldness of Mr. Agar's dramatic sense and the breadth of his vision lift us up to the grand movements of history. For readers of a later day this volume will be itself a historical document. Mr. Agar exploits the elusive living sources which die with the age itself: he has known personally, has seen the faces and heard the voices of many of the principal actors in his story, and he reacts to them as one living man to another. This is one of the reasons why this is not a "judicious" book. But it is also one of the reasons why this book is informed, intimate, impassioned, and persuasive.

Mr. Agar's point of view, popularly known as "internationalist," now happens to dominate both political parties. The student of American history need hardly be reminded that other men of no less good will and equally wide vision have believed otherwise. Even the reader who sees a different destiny for the United States cannot fail to reconsider his own version after reading this book, for Mr. Agar discovers many links between daily events and the largest historical questions.

Not himself an academic historian, Mr. Agar writes from the vantage point of journalism, publishing, and public affairs; he is in the great tradition of those who possess the historian's tools but whose workshop lies outside the university. He is peculiarly well qualified to bring the practical scholar's insights to the general reader, and so to serve the purposes of the "Chicago History of American Civilization." This series

Editor's Preface

contains two kinds of books: a *chronological* group which will provide a coherent narrative of American history from its beginning to the present day and a *topical* group which will deal with the history of varied and significant aspects of American life. Twenty-odd titles in the series are in preparation. Those which have already been published are listed at the end of this volume.

DANIEL J. BOORSTIN

Table of Contents

xi

Introduction

1

On the afternoon of April 12, 1945, Mr. Truman was in the office of Sam Rayburn, the Speaker of the House of Representatives. He was called on the telephone and asked to hurry to the White House. He assumed that President Franklin Roosevelt had come back to Washington for the funeral of a friend, Bishop Atwood, and that he wanted to question the Vice-President about problems in Congress before resuming his vacation. But the Vice-President was not taken to the executive offices. He was taken to Mrs. Roosevelt's study, where he learned that President Roosevelt had died suddenly in Georgia and that he, Harry Truman, was to be President of the United States. Stunned, he finally managed to ask: "Is there anything I can do for you?" "Is there anything *we* can do for *you?*" answered Mrs. Roosevelt. "For you are the one in trouble now."

The Price of Power

He was to learn abruptly the astonishing scale of that trouble. Within two hours, the Chief Justice had administered the oath of office, and the new President had held his first Cabinet meeting. When it adjourned, Secretary of War Stimson lingered behind to break the news about the atomic bomb.

The first experiment with a real bomb was still three months in the future. The men of science seemed to think it would work, but Admiral Leahy—Chief-of-Staff to the President from 1942 to 1949—was more reassuring. "This is the biggest fool thing we have done," he said. "The bomb will never go off, and I speak as an expert in explosives."

Aside from the weird and almost preposterous threat of the bomb and in spite of the shock of his new responsibilities, the world looked good to Mr. Truman (and, indeed, to most Americans) in April, 1945—better, perhaps, than it would ever look again. The Germans were about to collapse. There was no real awareness of the Russian menace; indeed, General Eisenhower was soon to write, after a trip to Moscow, that "nothing guides Russian policy so much as a desire for friendship with the United States." Japan, also, was clearly beaten, even though military and naval leaders predicted awe-inspiring casualties before she would admit her fate.

The mood of those carefree days was expressed by President Franklin Roosevelt in a message to Congress three months before he died: "This new year of 1945 can be the

Introduction

greatest year of achievement in human history. 1945 can see the final ending of the Nazi-Fascist reign of terror in Europe. 1945 can see the closing in of the forces of retribution about the center of the malignant power of imperialistic Japan. Most important of all—1945 can and must see the substantial beginning of the organization of world peace." And we have Mr. Truman's word that this was his view, too.

The American people, for the last time, were able to indulge the innocent illusion of "winning" a war—"winning," that is, in the sense that a contest between Arthurian knights might be won, with the names of the victors illuminated upon parchment, the survivors conducted triumphantly home, and the question at issue "settled." The miserable truth that world wars merely "settle" who is to carry the burden of civilization—briefly, until the next barbarian revolt—had not yet occurred to most of our people. But we know it now; a harsh lesson has been assimilated during ten harsh years. And the knowledge once gained can never be denied. Our long-preserved virginity of mind has at last been deflowered by the facts.

On the other side of the Atlantic, in that same April, Sir Winston Churchill[1] had no illusions and therefore no disillusions. He began the first decade of the atomic age with gloomy forebodings (gloomy even before he knew the bomb

1. Winston Churchill became a Knight of the Garter in 1953. For convenience and continuity he is referred to by his new title throughout.

was a "success"), and thus he ended it less troubled than many of our people. He described the world of 1945 as follows: "We can now see the deadly hiatus which existed between the fading of President Roosevelt's strength and the growth of President Truman's grip of the vast world problem. . . . The indispensable political direction was lacking at the moment when it was most needed. The United States stood on the scene of victory, master of world fortunes, but without a true and coherent design. . . . Thus this climax of apparently measureless success was to me a most unhappy time. I moved amid cheering crowds, or sat at a table adorned with congratulations and blessings from every part of the Grand Alliance, with an aching heart and a mind oppressed by forebodings."

How could America have "a true and coherent design" when she still believed that wars could be "won," that military success was a happy ending and not just another incident in an everlasting struggle? This great delusion had proved a handicap during the war itself. American intentions were often misunderstood because even our most friendly allies could not believe that we deliberately sacrificed the political ends of our effort to the military expediency of the moment. Because we were naïve about war, refusing to see it as "the most deadly form of politics," we were thrown off balance when we began to learn in 1946 how hollow a military victory can be. Our first feeling was that since we had won and

4

since the world was no safer, no easier, and scarcely more peaceful, this must be the work of traitors or of men so incompetent as to be no better than traitors. The anxieties and fears of our witch-hunting period may prove in the end to be no more than the by-products of growing up, of admitting to ourselves that peace cannot be won on the field of battle, and that for the powerful there is no security. Adolescence is always painful and often graceless. We may one day look back upon this crisis of our dawning maturity and compare the antics of Senator McCarthy to those of a wretched youth, bewildered by his surging emotions (or humiliated by too many pimples), who retaliates by setting fire to the henhouse and torturing the cat.

COMMIE SCARE

There was another reason why seemingly sane people were willing to listen to the McCarthys and the Jenners with their talk of treason in high places: we had long believed that the United States lived in a "safe" corner of the world—too far away to share the immemorial fears of other nations. Suddenly, with the outbreak of the Korean War, we discovered that we too were in perpetual danger: danger of defeat, danger of annihilation. This would seem natural to a European or an Asiatic, but to us it seemed unfair, out of order, unintended by Providence. Why should China, which we thought we had always befriended, pass into the hands of men who hated us? Why should Russia possess the bomb so quickly, when we had been told that the bomb would give us years of security? Why should we be at war in Asia, a war that we were not even allowed to win for fear of vaster troubles? Few people have ever been asked to enlarge their minds so fast, from the illusion of safety to the knowledge of danger.

If the world had only known us a little better or if currency restrictions had not prevented all but a few from traveling in America, those unseemly senators—those signs of our travail—would not have greatly harmed our reputation. If the world looks steadily at what we have learned in these ten years and at what we have done, it will find grounds for praise.

What a decade it has been: 1945, the bomb; 1946–47, total disillusionment with Russia, the Truman Doctrine, and the Marshall Plan; 1948–49, the Berlin airlift, the rape of Czechoslovakia, Communist victory in China; 1950–53, the Korean War (including general MacArthur, the war-within-a-war); 1951, desperate rearmament throughout the West; 1952–53, the American H-bomb followed by the Russian H-bomb; and, finally, in 1954–55, a little relaxation of tension?

2

If we discuss the first ten years of the atomic age in America against this background, we shall be writing chiefly about foreign politics. But are not all politics foreign politics today? Can we ever again (until we go the way of Carthage, Rome, and Spain) distinguish between parish politics and the affairs of mankind? The price of hogs, the "protection" afforded to wool or silver, the money to be spent on new schoolhouses—these are no longer problems for the corn-belt states, for Nevada and Colorado, or for the local parent-teacher association. The whole world is interested because the whole world needs our food, needs our markets, needs our money. And we need the whole world. There is nothing we can argue any more—except whether to cook tonight's corn "on the cob" or in a pudding—that is not afflicted with a global interest. (And, if we knew all the facts, we should doubtless find that Mr. Nehru has strong views about our evening meal.)

To take the most obvious example: when we write about the status of the Negro in the United States, we might seem to be discussing something essentially private—how a white man feels when his daughter goes to school in Kentucky, how a Negro feels when he pays too much rent in Harlem, how we all feel when we compare the American promise with the performance. If this isn't intimate, what is? Our own sins, our own hopes, our own failures, and our own belated triumphs? Yet the behavior of the white American toward his Negro fellow citizen and vice versa is more important to our foreign policy than any "summit meeting" could be or than most of the battles that we have won or lost. The world knows we are important and that we have to be heard politely at a conference. And the world knows we can fight, when we finally get around to it. But the world is perplexed as to whether we believe in what we grandly call "the American idea." The fate of many men and cities may depend on the world's decision in this matter.

So we can hardly order a new suit without taking part in foreign politics. And, for good or ill, such politics have become the most important of human activities, now that the men of science have digested the last of the hard core of their forbidden apple. While changing everything else, they have incidentally abolished our youthful American dream of a nation so happy and so harmless that it could "make do" with very little government. We know too much to be harmless ever again. We live in a diminished world of secrecy and "security," both of which depend on spies and permits and policemen and all forms of un-American activities.

"We have just enough religion to make us hate," wrote Dean Swift in the eighteenth century, "but not enough to make us love one another." To which we can now add: We have just enough science to put an end to the human race but not enough to feed and house the poor thing adequately and thus make it less pugnacious. Yet we have staggered through a decade of the atomic age, not without dignity. One of the chief architects of that age, Dr. Robert Oppenheimer—who has been forbidden access to "secret data" but whom we still rather daringly allow to tell himself what he is thinking— admits that "we have changed the face of the earth; we have changed the way we live; we may not change the condition of man's life but we have changed all the modes in which that condition occurs." In the face of this ultimate revolution, he says, "this is a world in which each of us will have to cling to what is close to him, to what he knows, to what he can do, to his friends and his tradition and his life, lest he be dissolved in a universal confusion and know nothing and love nothing."

This is good advice, and, on the whole, we have followed it. We can still know something and love something. And as long as that is true, we may have a future.

I

From San Francisco to Potsdam

1

President Truman, who had learned about the bomb during his first hours after taking office, learned also, during his first days, about Russian intransigence. Within a week he had reached the conclusion "that our agreements with the Soviet Union had so far been a one-way street and that this could not continue."

The second, the Russian, shock was almost as heavy as the first and almost as unexpected. Mr. Truman, having no experience of his own with Russia, had shared the cheerful views that were prevalent in Washington—a prevalence of hope, of lost, innocent, old-world hope, which is recaptured in the following quotation from Robert E. Sherwood: "The mood of the American delegates, including Roosevelt and Hopkins, could be described as one of supreme exultation as they left Yalta. . . . Hopkins later said to me, 'We really be-

lieved in our hearts that this was the dawn of the new day
we had all been praying for and talking about for so many
years. We were absolutely certain that we had won the first
great victory of the peace—and, by "we," I mean *all* of us, the
whole civilized human race. The Russians had proved that
they could be reasonable and farseeing and there wasn't any
doubt in the minds of the President or any of us that we could
live with them and get along with them peacefully for as far
into the future as any of us could imagine.' "

Sir Winston Churchill was less hopeful. He presented the
results of the Crimean conference to the House of Commons
as if these were friendly agreements among friendly allies.
Many members at once challenged him: Would the Russians
keep faith with Poland? "I decline absolutely," he replied
with some gloom, "to embark here on a discussion about
Russian good faith. . . . Sombre indeed would be the fortunes
of mankind if some awful schism arose between the Western
democracies and the Russian Soviet Union."

Even Franklin Roosevelt's hopefulness—which is the only
"crime" that can fairly be charged against him at Yalta—was
wearing thin by early March, two weeks after Sir Winston's
grim statement to Parliament. The President had named
Arthur Vandenberg, Republican senator from Michigan, as a
delegate to the coming conference at San Francisco—The
United Nations Conference on International Organization.
Vandenberg had many Polish constituents and a warm ro-

mantic feeling for Poland, "both for her own precious sake," as he wrote, "and as a symbol." He spoke harshly in the Senate on the injustice of the Russian treatment of Poland during the brief weeks since Yalta. He thus became a prime "imperialist beast" to the press and radio of Moscow, and he asked President Roosevelt whether he should withdraw as a delegate. "We have to deal with the Russians," he said, "and I don't want to make it difficult. I can conveniently arrange to break a leg—if you wish." Roosevelt answered, "Just between us, Arthur, I am coming to know the Russians better, and if I could name only one delegate to the San Francisco Conference, you would be that delegate."

Thus perished the lighthearted American hope of getting along with the Russians "for as far into the future as any of us could imagine." Because it was lighthearted and thus unexamined, it died of the first contention, bequeathing the poison of frustrated good will. Had the hope been based coldly upon the facts of power, it might at least have survived one decade of the atomic dispensation. The United States, in that case, might have seemed less amiable but also less dangerous. We have often frightened the postwar world—friends and foes alike—because we are not yet inured to the disenchantment that attends upon greatness. We hope too much and hate too quickly. Time will cure us of that; but must time also water our ardor, corrupt our talent for believing three improbable things before breakfast? Or can we mingle experience with enthusiasm: the poet's secret, the secret of the Greeks and of the English?

Mr. Truman, from his first day in office, never lacked for lessons in disenchantment. When he called Soviet-American relations a "one-way street," he had such facts as these in mind. The Yalta conference ended on February 11, 1945. The Russians had agreed that democratic governments should be set up in eastern Europe. Hardly had the conference dispersed, when Mr. Vishinsky arrived in Bucharest to impose upon Rumania a government under Communist domination. The same was soon to happen in Bulgaria, in Hungary, and—most important of all from the British and American point of view—in Poland. Many Britons felt strongly and conscientiously about Poland (they had gone to war to save her); and so did many Americans feel strongly and tenderly, not only because of the Polish population in the United States, but also from a tradition of sympathy for Poland's repeated woes and of admiration for Poland's valor.

On April 22, ten days after the death of Roosevelt and three days before the opening of the San Francisco conference, Mr. Molotov called on President Truman, who at once raised the question of Russia's intentions toward Poland. "I pointed out," he writes, "that in its larger aspects the Polish question had become for our people the symbol of the future development of our international relations."

Mr. Truman was saying that if Russia meant to betray the

13

The Price of Power

Poles and in the name of Yalta to associate the United States with this deed, America might think twice before accepting her place among the United Nations. But the Russians knew better than Mr. Truman. They knew it was too late to play the cards of 1919. They knew that the United States in 1945 could no more lay aside her burdensome powers than Atlas could let slip the sky. They knew, therefore, that no matter how long or bitterly we bargained, we should have to accept the best "deal" we could get for Poland, short of another war. So Molotov answered the President evasively.

The next day, in a meeting with Secretary of State Stettinius and with the British foreign secretary, Molotov showed his hand blandly and cynically, insisting that the agreements on Poland were being carried out to the letter—whereas Russia had already created her puppet government in Poland and was confident that she could force the *fait accompli* upon the United States and Great Britain. Nevertheless, as a sign of the trap in which the West was caught, General Marshall and Mr. Stimson, the Secretary of War, warned the President against too much firmness on the Polish question, lest the Russians break the most important of their promises at Yalta and refrain from fighting Japan.

Mr. Truman's idea of "too much" firmness was perhaps not quite that of his advisers. In the final interview before Molotov left for San Francisco, the President replied sharply at each effort to gloss over the Polish question, saying "that an agreement had been reached and that there was only one thing to do, and that was for Marshal Stalin to carry out that agreement in accordance with his word."

"I have never been talked to like that in my life," Molotov said.

"Carry out your agreements," Mr. Truman answered, "and you won't get talked to like that!"

2

A few days later, at San Francisco, Molotov showed that he was unimpressed. He very nearly destroyed the United Nations Organization while it was still unborn by nullifying another of the decisions made at Yalta. Everyone had there agreed that each permanent member of the Security Council[1] should be allowed to veto the use of war or of sanctions against itself. This veto, however, did not extend to the mere discussion of a complaint against a permanent member. Molotov now insisted that it did, and the conference ground to a halt.

Luckily, Harry Hopkins—Roosevelt's fabulous alter ego and diplomatic errand boy—had already been sent to Moscow to argue face to face with Stalin about the Poles. He got nowhere on the Polish question, but when he asked about the veto, Stalin made no trouble at all. Molotov had been thumb-

1. The permanent seats on the Security Council were to be held by the United States, Great Britain, the Soviet Union, France, and China. The remaining six seats were to be held by other nations for two-year terms.

ing his nose at President Truman, and Stalin told him to stop.
So the Charter of the United Nations was signed on June 26
and was ratified in the American Senate by a vote of 89 to 2.

While Harry Hopkins was earning high credit for break-
ing the deadlock at Moscow, the most forceful and effective
of the Americans at San Francisco was his old isolationist
critic, Arthur Vandenberg of Michigan. The benefits which
this inexplicable man, this most generous of converts, con-
ferred upon his country during the next five years cannot be
overestimated. The danger is that they may be partly forgotten. Many of them are hard to document, since they depend upon the power of personal example. Those of us who
watched him in action should therefore testify while there is
still time, especially since he died at the height of his powers
and of his usefulness to the world.

Vandenberg had been the isolationists' favorite candidate
for the Republican presidential nomination in 1940. When
the Lend-Lease Bill passed the Senate in March, 1941, with
a vote of 60 to 31, he wrote in his diary: "If America 'cracks
up' you can put your finger on this precise moment as the
time when the crime was committed. . . . I doubt if *all* those
who supported it [Lend-Lease] realized its implications. I
hope I am wholly wrong when I say I fear they will live to
regret their votes beyond anything else they ever did. I had
the feeling, as the result of the ballot was announced, that I
was witnessing the suicide of the Republic." Even after Pearl
Harbor and after the German and Italian declarations of war

against the United States, Vandenberg argued (with much reason) that a Senate resolution was inaccurate which said that war had been "thrust" upon the United States. "If this *Van* war is worth fighting," he wrote, "it is worth accepting for what it is—namely, a belligerent cause which we openly embraced long ago and in which we long since *nominated ourselves* as active participants. The 'thrusting' started two years ago when we repealed the arms embargo."

Nevertheless, in spite of his fears for the Republic, in spite of his distrust for all the policies of Franklin Roosevelt, Vandenberg recognized Pearl Harbor as the end of a long cycle of American history, the end of his hope that the future might resemble the past. "My convictions," he wrote, "regarding international co-operation and collective security for peace took firm form on the afternoon of the Pearl Harbor attack. That day ended isolationism for any realist." These new "convictions" of the Senator were to become a mighty influence on America's postwar politics. It is doubtful whether the great decisions of Mr. Truman's administrations could have been made at all without the help of this reformed Republican isolationist. It is certain that they could not have been made with such near-unanimity.

3

At the close of the San Francisco conference Mr. Truman had reached only the first stage of disillusionment with Russia, the stage of saying: "But you *made* these agreements, didn't you? You *signed* them. Why on earth don't you *keep* them? Then everything would be all right." This is what he kept saying, uselessly, to Molotov. This is what Harry Hopkins, who had risen from a sickbed that was practically a deathbed to make his last effort for his country, begged Stalin to believe was the mood of America. He reminded the Marshal how they had first met in 1941, when the Russian armies were in flight before the Germans, and how the Marshal had convinced him that Russia would fight forever if necessary— fight all the way back to central Asia if necessary—and how he, Hopkins, had gone home and persuaded Roosevelt that this was true, with the result that Roosevelt had ignored the experts who told him the German armies must soon be in Moscow and had put through a program of aid to Russia.

Stalin admitted, frigidly, that Hopkins had come to the right conclusions in 1941.

Then why on earth, said Hopkins, do you insist on making your friends look silly today? Millions of Americans would like to believe in Russia's good faith. But they feel betrayed. Poland is only one unhappy example. Our crossed purposes are beginning to seem world-wide. And why? "I told Stalin," wrote Hopkins, "that . . . I was bewildered with some of the things that were going on."

Hopkins was "bewildered," at least in part, because he had believed that the promises made at Yalta would remain binding on the Russians, whether or not there was any power in western Europe to enforce them. This was foolish enough;

From San Francisco to Potsdam

but Hopkins also seemed to believe that a simple American threat to withdraw from the world stage might frighten Stalin. He then used the argument that President Truman had tried so unsuccessfully on Molotov. He said that the Russian behavior toward Poland might decide whether the United States would take part in world affairs or whether she would withdraw into her ancient solitude. In other words: "Be good! Do just what we want! Or we shall run away and leave you to your own devices!"

This was like threatening to throw a rump steak to a dog if he didn't stop barking. But Stalin knew that the threat was too good to be true. His answer, according to Hopkins, was that "whether the United States wished it or not, it was a world power and would have to accept world interests."

The record of the talks between Hopkins and Stalin is fascinating and deplorable; it displays the tragedy of the postwar decade, for it shows a minimum of understanding, both ways. Hopkins was still asking, "What has gone wrong?" He did not even know that part of the answer could be found in any copy of the American Army newspaper, *Stars and Stripes*. How would an audience of GI's have received Hopkins, now that Germany was defeated, had he stopped off on his way to Moscow to tell them that they must remain for years in Europe because the Russians were unkind to Poles and Bulgarians? How would an audience of American parents have received him had he made the same speech before setting out from home?

The Price of Power

The men in the Kremlin knew the answers to these questions. They had always been told that democracies were soft and self-regarding. And here were the Americans, helpless before a stampede for demobilization, yet continuing to talk as if they disposed of power in Europe. Within a few months, negotiations between Americans and Russians on the fate of eastern Europe would be on a par with negotiations between rabbits and weasels—except that a rabbit rarely stamps his foot and says that if the weasels don't look out, he'll go away.

A prudent ruler, wrote Machiavelli, "ought not to keep faith when by doing so it would be against his interest and when the reasons which made him bind himself no longer exist." It was against Russia's interest to have eastern Europe in the hands of Westernized democratic governments, such as the renascent government of Czechoslovakia. The "reasons which made her bind herself" to such an arrangement were chiefly the American and British armies, and, so far as eastern Europe was concerned, these would soon "no longer exist." So, thought the Russians, what is all the fuss about? After all, it was a dean of the Church of England who wrote that "promises and pie-crust are made to be broken."

Harry Hopkins—perhaps to his honor but not to his credit as a statesman—did not think in such terms. Sherwood quotes a charming, pathetic note that Hopkins handed to the President during the final meeting at Yalta. The Russians had been claiming that they should receive ten billion dollars in reparations from Germany, and the British had been raising objections. Hopkins wrote: "The Russians have given in so much at this conference that I don't think we should let them down. Let the British disagree if they want to—and continue their disagreement at Moscow." ✓

"I don't think we should let them down." This was what Stalin was incapable of understanding—just as Hopkins had forgotten, or had never read, his Machiavelli. If the Marshal had seen this note, he might well have thought it some devious trick. The Russians have their Marxian textbook that explains all human conduct, but the textbook has no chapter on innocence. The more innocently or naïvely we behave, the more incomprehensible we become to the Russians. They can only assume that our real motives are even worse than they expected, since our apparent motives make no sense.

The Russians, locked in their Asiatic prison, could scarcely be asked to understand Americans, but we have no excuse for not understanding the relation between power and policy. Since Western strength could not be maintained in Europe from 1945 to 1947, since this was politically impossible, we might at least have modified our rage when Russian strength (unimpaired by "getting the boys home") obeyed the normal laws of nature and flowed into the vacuum we had left behind us. Why should we be the first people in history to have our cake and eat it too—our soldiers demobilized and our far-flung interests guarded?

4

What did we really think would happen when we left Europe? Did we think the Russians had become conservatives because Stalin had begun to talk about the "Fatherland war" —the name of Czar Alexander's war against Napoleon? In some ways we had more to fear from them as conservatives than as revolutionaries. For two hundred years Russia had been pushing at those eastern gates of Europe, seeking to dominate the millions who live between the Baltic and the Black Sea. Again and again she got at least one foot inside the door. She had been ejected with difficulty after the Napoleonic Wars. She had been ejected again after the Treaty of San Stefano, and deprived of her Balkan spoils by the Congress of Berlin. Surely, Stalin was not a villain but merely a Russian when he continued this ancient pressure and revived this old dream of czarist diplomacy? This time, however, there would be no one to eject the Muscovites, "the Turks of the North," as they had long been called. We planned, quite simply, to destroy the German armies and to withdraw the British and American armies; so what did we expect the Russians to do?

We had no illusions as to Russia's future strength. The illusions had to do with the use she would make of that strength. At the first Quebec conference, in August, 1943, an American military estimate on "Russia's Position" was presented. This was realistic in its facts and childish in its deductions. "Russia's post-war position in Europe will be a dominant one," said the document. "With Germany crushed, there is no power in Europe to oppose her tremendous military forces. The conclusions from the foregoing are obvious. Since Russia is the decisive factor in the war, she must be given every assistance and every effort must be made to obtain her friendship. Likewise, since without question she will dominate Europe on the defeat of the Axis, it is even more essential to develop and maintain the most friendly relations with Russia."

"Friendly relations"? These would be easy to maintain so long as nobody opposed, first, Russia's dominance over eastern Europe, including eastern Germany, and, second, her dominance over the whole of Germany as soon as the time came to end the four-power occupation. As we have said, centuries of history lay back of these ambitions. Long before the modern instances that we have mentioned—in fact, ever since 967, when the Eastern Roman emperor had unwisely called Prince Svyatoslav of Russia to his aid—these people had been pressing toward Constantinople and toward the West.

And why not? The West was relatively rich, well endowed by nature, and with a climate most benign compared to the fierce eastern plains. If the West could not protect herself, someone would absorb her. Since the days of Charlemagne she had been fighting off the Russians and Mohammedans—and until the eighteenth century the one had had about as much relation to Europe as the other; for Russia, historic Russia, owed nothing to Latin culture except what dribbled eastward through Byzantium, and she was little affected by the great crises of Western history, such as the Renaissance, the Reformation, the discovery of the New World, the American and French revolutions. She was not an outpost of the West; she was something different, indigenous, in her own right. She did not want to become an adjunct of the West; but when her time came she wanted to take it over. And by 1943 her time seemed to be coming, which is why "friendly relations" were not the answer.

But was there any answer at all? We must try to come to terms with this question before we can hope to understand the internal and external troubles of the United States during the postwar decade.

In theory, had we been dealing with things rather than with people, the answer would have been to maintain Western strength at its maximum at all times—to move straight from Potsdam, let us say, to NATO at its strongest. This was politically impossible. The Communists were the strongest party in France and Italy. And no American President or British Prime Minister could have opposed demobilization until Russia had been given several years to prove to the general public that her ambitions were very great, were dangerous to the West, and were implacable. Communism enters the picture with the phrase "dangerous to the West," since communism plays a vital part in the techniques of the cold war. But, on the whole, we shall see our problems more clearly if we think of Russia (a great power with a great historic drive) rather than if we think of communism, which was born yesterday and is difficult to define.

A second answer, which has been put forward since the war by many disgruntled Americans and Englishmen, seems equally impossible to those who remember the mood of 1943–45. This answer was to "save" Germany as a bulwark against the East by making an early peace that would, so the argument runs, have destroyed the power of the Nazis but not the power of Germany to resist Russia. A few months before the Quebec conference the Spanish foreign minister put this view strongly to Sir Samuel Hoare, British ambassador in Spain. "Which is the greater danger," asked Count Jordana, "not only for the continent but for England herself, a Germany not totally defeated and with sufficient strength to serve as a rampart against Communism . . . or a Sovietized Germany which would certainly furnish Russia with the added strength of her war preparations, her engineers, her specialized workmen and technicians? . . . If Germany did not exist, Europeans would have to invent her."

Again, this was a policy that might have been imposed upon things but that could not be offered, at least in the Western world, to people. It leaves out of account that world's distaste for Germany toward the end of the war. By this time Germany had "solved" the Jewish problem by killing the six million Jews at her disposal, and she had kept her ovens warm in order to "solve" the Polish problem in the same way. By this time she had killed at least ten million Russians, of whom six to seven million may have been soldiers—but even the killing of soldiers makes for bad feeling. By this time the vast charnel-dumps of concentration camps, which the Germans never noticed in their own fair countryside, had been noticed by many foreigners and had been reluctantly accepted as impossible but true by a shivering Western world. Such deeds make for indignation, and by 1945 Westerners were not in a reasonable mood about Germany. Perhaps the Russians were not wholly dispassionate either; but within that despotic state there may have been a power strong enough to turn the war off, had such a policy seemed wise. There was no such power in the West. Heaven help the politician who had tried to explain that in order to frustrate the Russians, who were doing too well against Germany, we were planning to break our repeated promises and and make a separate, lenient peace. (The Russians, incidentally, were afraid until the very end of the war that we would do exactly this.)

Not only were the Germans unpopular, but the Russians, as so many of us seem to forget, were extremely well thought of during the years of the war. In a book published in 1942, the present author referred to Russia as "an Asiatic tyranny."

From San Francisco to Potsdam

He was taken to task on the front page of the *New York Times Book Review* for underestimating the virtues of our great ally. Things are as they are and not as we would like them to be. And things were as they were, and it is a poor service to democratic politics to distort reality in order to pretend that our present problems would never have arisen if someone had only done what, in fact, was impossible.

There is another, a military, suggestion as to how we might have diminished the threat of Russian postwar dominance over eastern and central Europe. Major General J. F. C. Fuller, among others, makes a most compelling argument for this suggestion. "After the successful landing [in Normandy] on June 6th," he writes, "in any set of circumstances the defeat of Germany was assured in the immediate future; the time had come to suit strategy to policy. . . . The backbone of the decisive political theatre remained the line Vienna-Prague-Berlin. Were the western allies the first to gain that line, in spite of their purblind commitments at Teheran they would still be able largely to shape the eventual peace; but were the Russians to do so, then, faced by Russia's military might, they would be compelled to toe the line."

This appears to have been the view of Sir Winston Churchill and the British chiefs-of-staff, when in August, 1944, they asked the Americans not to wreck General Alexander's Italian campaign by withdrawing 100,000 men for a seemingly needless invasion of the south of France. If not thus weakened, they said, General Alexander could push forward into the Po Valley, into Istria and Trieste and the Ljubjana gap, thereby threatening an area vital to the enemy—and also vital to the Russians if they were to control eastern, middle, and southern Europe. But the British request was refused by the Americans. General Eisenhower was against their plan. The American Chiefs-of-Staff were against it. And, acting on the advice of his generals, the President was against it. Sir Winston sadly notes that "we had now passed the day in July [1944] when . . . the movement of the great American armies into Europe and their growth in the Far East made their numbers in action for the first time greater than our own. Influence on allied operations is usually increased by large reinforcements."

General Alexander's armies were duly deprived. Southern and eastern and central Europe was left to the Russians. And the decision was made not by political friends of Russia but by American generals who had not been taught to think of war in terms of politics. So it is fair to say that this plan, too, was impossible—which means that there was no answer, during the war, to the problem of postwar Russia. We had to wait and see, and suffer, and do our best, and try to patch up as many of the inevitable weak spots as could be patched. ✓ The reader may ask, What does this argument suggest about democracy? Is it true that a democratic state or an alliance of such states cannot face reality when reality becomes harsh? If we are too selfish to keep up our strength when the shooting is over, too emotional to take the long view of Germany and forgive her sensational crimes, and too innocent to understand that a war is not worth winning if its political purpose is sacrificed to military expediency, can we in fact survive? But is not this question the meaning and the drama of modern history? This is what we are here to prove, one way or another. No one has a right to answer "Yes" or "No" until the question has been explored to its conclusion. ✓

We may admit that no democracy in the past has lasted long, but we may add in fairness that its repeated failures to survive have been followed by repeated resurrections. We may even boast that in the testing days since Potsdam the free world has not done badly. But any boast must be made with humility, in the shadow of two great fears: the bomb, which may make all questions and all answers idle, and the fact that in desperate times democracy is subject to the danger that evil men may seize power by persuading anxious, decent people that the times need not be bad at all, that the nation has simply been betrayed.

5

Before turning to Potsdam, where the American leaders discovered the second phase of disillusion—no longer "Why don't they keep their promises?" but rather "Are there any bounds to their ambitions?"—let us list exactly what was agreed at Yalta, or what was "given away," as the myth has it.

Some of the agreements at Yalta remained secret until after the war. The Germans and the Japanese were still undefeated, and it might have been unwise to tell them just what we planned for their destruction. The price of such "open diplomacy" might have been tens of thousands of lives, and the dead men's ghosts might have wondered. Yet the secrecy made it possible for Senator Robert A. Taft to say that "the unauthorized agreements made at Yalta . . . set up Soviet Russia in a position where it dominates Europe and Asia today."

Russian power, however, would have dominated nothing, harmed nobody, if the agreements made at Yalta had been kept. What further agreements would Taft have recommended for the Russians to violate?

The debatable decisions at Yalta dealt either with Poland or with Russia's entry into the war against Japan. Poland was discussed at seven out of the eight plenary meetings of the conference. It was soon agreed that the eastern boundary should be the Curzon line.[2] After endless argument, the west-

2. This was the eastern frontier recognized by the Allies in December, 1919. It was roughly the frontier of Napoleon's Duchy of Warsaw, which perished with the Grand Army in the retreat from Moscow in 1812. The line ran north along the river Bug, from the old frontier of Austria-Hungary to beyond Brest-Litovsk, then north again to Grodno and the present Lithuanian border. After her victory over Russia in 1920–21, Poland rashly pushed her frontier far eastward, absorbing about seven million non-Poles. In 1940, when Poland was again partitioned between Germany and Russia, the U.S.S.R. returned to the Curzon line.

ern boundary was left to a future peace conference. The Russians wanted it where it is today, on the western Neisse, whereas the British and the Americans wanted it much farther east. Russia, whose vast armies were investing the country at the time of the Yalta conference, regarded Poland as her property. She wished it, therefore, to contain as much of Germany as possible. Roosevelt and Sir Winston Churchill disagreed; but, short of risking a new war while the old war was still raging, what could they have done except postpone the issue?

Even more troublesome than Poland's boundaries was the question of Poland's new government. The Lublin government, Russian-sponsored, was already in existence and on the spot. The London government-in-exile was also vociferously in existence, but far from home. Yet the Poles in London represented, at the very least, an army of 150,000 men who had fought heroically beside the British. The Poles at Lublin represented what? Nobody in the West could discover. Nobody in the West was allowed to go to see. Sir Winston Churchill stated the problem, to which he well knew there was no answer: "If the conference is to brush aside the existing London Government and lend all its weight to the Lublin Government there will be a world outcry. . . . All our differences will of course be removed if a free and unfettered General Election is held in Poland by ballot and with universal suffrage and free candidatures. Once this is done His Majesty's Government will salute the Government that emerges without regard to the Polish Government in London."

Except for the fact that he had no Polish government-in-exile to deal with at Washington, this represents President Roosevelt's point of view. Neither he nor Sir Winston wished to force the London Poles upon the Poles at home. Like all exiles, the Poles in London had been most troublesome; but they represented a noble element in a noble nation, and the British and Americans had pledged themselves that the liberated peoples would have a free choice as to their future leaders. Yet what could be done?

Stalin said that, of course, he wanted the Poles to have free elections, but the war had so far interfered. "How soon," asked Roosevelt, "will it be possible to hold elections?" "Within a month," said Stalin, "unless there is some catastrophe on the front, which is improbable."

So it was agreed that the Lublin government was to be "reorganized on a wider democratic basis, with the inclusion of democratic leaders from Poland itself, and also from those living abroad." This reorganized government was to hold free elections "as soon as possible."

Perhaps Mr. Roosevelt believed all this talk about elections; he is said to have told Sir Winston that the differences between the Western allies and the Russians were now largely a matter of words. But suppose nobody believed it, what could the Americans or the British do? Stalin had made the necessary minimum of promises. If we did not believe even the minimum, should we have asked him to promise a lot more? We had nothing with which to threaten, no sanctions to invoke. The Russians were still killing more Germans every day than all the rest of us put together, and we still desperately wanted their help in the war against Japan. Should we have told them—as the intransigent Poles were always preaching—that as soon as we had destroyed Hitler, we would go to war with Stalin? Would the private soldier in the American or British armies have welcomed the news that, instead of making "unauthorized agreements at Yalta," we had saved Taft's conscience and split with the Russians, who were therefore content to stand on the Neisse and let a hundred and twenty German divisions move west? And what about the million Americans who we still thought might be expended in the Pacific unless the Russians joined that war as well?

These are not rhetorical questions. We can make no sense out of the first decade of our postwar history unless they are faced rigorously.

The promises in regard to Poland—a democratic government, free elections, and so on—were extended at Yalta to all the victims of Germany in a "Declaration on Liberated Europe"; "unconditional surrender" was reaffirmed; the conference at San Francisco to create the United Nations Charter was convened; and it was secretly agreed that America would support the proposal that the Ukraine and Byelorussia be given membership in the United Nations as independent states. The latter promise was not exacted by Russian strength in Europe but by Japanese strength in Manchuria.

6

General MacArthur was confident that a large-scale invasion of Japan would be necessary before the emperor could be brought to surrender. General Marshall agreed. The American Chiefs-of-Staff agreed. They were all therefore eager to see the Soviet Union enter the Pacific war, especially since the largest and the best of Japan's armies was on the Asian mainland, in Manchuria. If Russia could attack this army and prevent it from returning home, she might help to save a million American lives and half that number of British —Sir Winston Churchill's estimate of the lives saved by the use of the atomic bomb and the consequent capitulation of Japan.

There were military men, of course, who thought that Japan was close to surrender in 1945, with or without Russia, with or without the bomb; but they were in a small minority. All the experience of the war so far suggested that the Japanese had an abnormal relish for dying to the last man—dying long after death served any useful purpose, but taking a terrible toll of American soldiers and marines in the meanwhile. For example, eight days after the Yalta conference ended, the

From San Francisco to Potsdam

United States Marines invaded Iwo Jima, an island so tiny that, until it acquired its present grisly fame, it could not even be shown by a dot on the map. The island was taken after six weeks of fighting. The Marines lost 4,189 killed, 15,308 wounded, 441 missing. Then, on the first of April, Okinawa was invaded—an object at least large enough to see. It was taken after almost three months of fighting. The Americans lost 11,260 killed and 33,769 wounded. If the home islands of Japan were to be defended with a similar tenacity, if the Japanese were to fight as the British would have fought under Sir Winston Churchill's leadership, from the beaches to the hills and from house to house in every town, the Churchillian estimate of a million and a half dead invaders does not seem implausible.

Such, in any case, were the prevailing fears in 1945. As late as July 25, twelve days before the bomb fell on Hiroshima, Alexander Wiley, Republican senator from Wisconsin, was pleading in the American Senate for the Russians to enter the war. "In millions of homes," he said, "mothers, fathers and sweethearts are waiting anxiously for news of Russia's intentions." And, according to Secretary of State Stettinius, "Even as late as the Potsdam conference, after the first atomic bomb had exploded on July 16th, the military insisted that the Soviet Union be brought into the Far Eastern war. At both Yalta and Potsdam, the military staffs were particularly concerned with the Japanese troops in Manchuria. Described as the cream of the Japanese army, this self-contained force, with its own autonomous command, and industrial base, was believed capable of prolonging the war even after the islands of Japan had been subdued." 57 2 8

The Russians, presumably, understood all this. In view of the strength of their bargaining position, they might have been far more demanding. The plain fact was that we Americans wanted to buy their army; so we had to pay the market price.

In Europe, as we have seen, the price was British and American support for the membership of the Ukraine and of Byelorussia in the United Nations. This was a genuine concession, for it was something Russia could not take by force either before or after the peace. In Asia, however, Stalin asked for nothing to which he could not at any time have helped himself: the return of southern Sakhalin and the transfer of the Kuriles, the internationalization of Dairen in Manchuria, a lease of Port Arthur as a naval base, the joint Soviet-Chinese operation of the Manchurian railways, an occupation zone in Korea, a recognition by the United States and Great Britain of the autonomy of outer Mongolia, which had already severed its connections with China and come under Soviet influence. In return, Stalin promised to enter the Japanese war and to make a treaty of friendship and alliance with Chiang Kai-shek's Nationalist regime.

Both these Russian promises were kept. The treaty that

Stalin made with Chiang accorded to the latter full recognition as the ruler of China. It is possible that Stalin, also, was at this time taken in by Chiang and thought him capable of building a true national state. At least, the treaty gave Chiang his chance. It was saluted in *Life* magazine under the heading, "The Moscow Treaty Gives China Her First Real Chance To Complete an Old Revolution."

7

The meeting at Potsdam began on July 17, 1945. America had just abandoned the last chance to put pressure on the Russians for the salvation of eastern Europe. This was not the work of fellow travelers in Washington but of General Eisenhower and his commanders in the field, the Chiefs-of-Staff agreeing. British protests were overridden by President Truman, who refused to interfere with his generals. According to these generals, war was too serious to be hampered by politics. It should be fought for its own sake, and let the future look after itself.

At the time of Roosevelt's death, the diplomatic situation in Europe was described as follows by Sir Winston Churchill: "Every question about the future was unsettled. . . . The agreements and understandings at Yalta, such as they were, had already been broken or brushed aside by the triumphant Kremlin. New perils, perhaps as terrible as those we had surmounted, loomed and glared upon the torn and harassed world." In the face of these "new perils," the Western Allies had one unexpected advantage: the British and American armies were advancing through Germany with unforeseen speed. They had already moved far beyond the lines of occupation agreed upon with the Russians.

"This raised the question," writes Mr. Truman, "of how far east our armies should go, what lines they should hold when the fighting stopped, and the relation of all this to the occupation zones. Churchill, on political grounds, pressed for getting a line as far to the east as possible before the fighting ended. Opposed to this policy were our military chiefs, whose arguments were based on military grounds."

Sir Winston never suggested that the agreements in regard to zones should not ultimately prevail. He wanted the Western armies to move east as far as possible and then to sit stubbornly while the bargaining with Russia took place. The armies would be withdrawn whenever Russia held the promised free elections in Poland, agreed to the promised division of zones in Austria, and allowed the Allies free access to the liberated countries.

On April 30 Sir Winston told President Truman: "There can be little doubt that the liberation of Prague and as much as possible of the territory of Western Czechoslovakia by your forces might make the whole difference to the post-war situation in Czechoslovakia, and might well influence that in near-by countries. . . . If the Western Allies play no significant part in Czechoslovakian liberation, that country will go the way of Yugoslavia." He added that he was not telling General Eisenhower how to run the war but that "the highly important political considerations mentioned above" should not be neglected.

They were totally neglected, however, and on military grounds. "Highly important political considerations" were not of interest to our generals. An earlier British attempt to get Western troops into Berlin ahead of the Russians was countered by General Eisenhower in the following message to Washington: "May I point out that Berlin is no longer a particularly important objective." Mr. Truman comments: "Our Chiefs of Staff supported Eisenhower." Yet in 1948, at the time of the incredible airlift, the Administration thought Berlin worth holding at the risk of world-wide ruin.

Perhaps because of his minor military experience in World War I, Mr. Truman had a veneration for generals. He really seemed to think that they knew more than other people. His own answer to the new perils that "loomed and glared upon the torn and harassed world" was guileless: "If they [the Russians] were firm in their way," he writes, "we could be firm in ours. And our way was to stick to our agreements and keep insisting that they do the same." Insisting? The word is impressive; but what do you insist with, if your generals overawe you when it comes to occupying the politically important spots and if your voters overawe you when it comes to maintaining an army? Potsdam supplied the answer: You don't insist; you take what you can get and pretend to like it.

When the German war ended on May 8, 1945, the Western armies had penetrated beyond their zones of occupation on a front 400 miles in length and at one point 120 miles in depth. This was less than we might have accomplished, but it was still something. Should we abandon even this last bargaining point? Should we go naked to Potsdam, clad only in honor: "We have kept all our promises; we have given you every chance to savage our friends; we 'insist' that you treat them gently"? This time the generals could not be blamed. The war was over in Europe, and the President's decisions had to be made by the President himself.[3]

On May 12, four days after the surrender, Sir Winston sent his "iron-curtain" telegram to Mr. Truman; it was one of the great state papers of modern history, but had no effect.

". . . What is to happen about Russia?" asked Sir Winston. ". . . What will be the position in a year or two, when the British and American Armies have melted and the French has not yet been formed on any major scale, when we may have a handful of divisions, mostly French, and when Russia may choose to keep two or three hundred on active service?

"An iron curtain is drawn down upon their front. We do not know what is going on behind. There seems little doubt

3. The Americans now had about three million troops in Europe, the British about one million. So the Americans called the tune.

that the whole of the regions east of the line Lübeck-Trieste-Corfu will soon be completely in their hands. To this must be added the further enormous area conquered by the American armies between Eisenach and the Elbe, which will, I suppose, in a few weeks be occupied, when the Americans retreat, by the Russian power. . . . Thus a broad band of many hundreds of miles of Russian-occupied territory will isolate us from Poland. . . .

"Surely it is vital now to come to an understanding with Russia, or see where we are with her, before we weaken our armies mortally or retire to the zones of occupation."

There it is: the theme of postwar history is displayed in brief, and an answer to the looming danger is proposed. Nobody listened. "To give up the whole centre and heart of Germany—nay, the centre and keystone of Europe—as an isolated act, seemed to me a grave and improvident decision." Thus spoke Sir Winston Churchill in retrospect. He was the only man in high authority who also said it in prospect. We may all now admit it to have been grave and improvident, but such was the decision. And it was an American decision. Until the last hour of the last day, the British kept asking that the armies of the West should remain in their forward position until Potsdam, until Stalin could be consulted face to face. Mr. Truman replied that it would harm our relations with the Soviet Union to postpone action until July. He ordered all American troops to begin their withdrawal on June 21.

The Price of Power

Obviously, we shall not know in our lifetime whether Mr. Truman was right or wrong. He is not so simple a man as he likes to pretend, and the problem was not so simple as he presents it. In his *Memoirs* he talks only about "our relation with the Soviet" or with the British. Far more important to the future of mankind was his own relation with the American people, which he does not mention. During the next few years this strange little man—lively and pert to the verge of bumptiousness; more widely read in history than any President since John Quincy Adams; more wilful than any President since James K. Polk; more incompetent in dividing the good from the bad among his own friends at home than any President since Warren Harding—would make and enforce a series of decisions upon which, for better or for worse, our world now rests, or shakes. ✓

An American President, however, can "enforce" nothing unless the people support him. The constitutional duty (and the daily delight) of the Congress is to insure that the President's powers shall not be augmented. The interest of the opposition press (which in Mr. Truman's case was nine papers out of ten) is to make the President look as silly as possible. He has no friends but the people. Let us assume that he thought the people were doomed unless they could gather their strength and their abiding resolution to oppose Russia. Was it better to ask for this opposition in the seemingly happy days, in the first flush of victory before Potsdam? Or was it better to stand defenseless and allow the people to watch Russian diplomacy at work? Did Mr. Truman, in other words, choose to go naked to Potsdam, knowing that the Russians would call vulgar attention to his bareness and laugh at his shield of honor? Or was he simply taken in by generals who thought war more important than the purposes for which it is fought? We shall never know—we, who have watched him at work with such mingled emotions for so many years. To us, there are at least three Mr. Trumans, and we wonder how the historians of the future will squeeze them all into the same skin.

8

Whatever the President's motives for his decisions in April and May and June, the Western democracies went naked to Potsdam. And empty-handed they returned—not only empty-handed but conscience-stricken, because of the final betrayal of Poland. The West, to be sure, was in no position to prevent Poland from being robbed and then castrated and then branded on the forehead with the hammer and sickle—all this as an epilogue to mass murder, first by our enemies and then by our allies. But the inevitable may still be lamented.

Let us remember that Poland was only the symbol. There were other countries that had served freedom and that were also sacrificed to the inability of the West to face Russia in 1945. Major General Fuller describes the Europe that was provisionally agreed upon at Potsdam in these words:

The Price of Power

"Stalin, the supreme realist, whose strategy had throughout kept in step with his policy, had been able to impose his messianic cult upon Estonia, Latvia, Lithuania, part of Finland, Poland, eastern and central Germany, a third of Austria, Czechoslovakia, Yugoslavia, Hungary, Rumania and Bulgaria. Vienna, Prague and Berlin, the vertebrae of Europe, were his, and, except for Athens, so was every capital city in eastern Europe. The western frontier of Russia had been advanced from the Pripet Marshes to the Thüringerwald, a distance of 750 miles, and, as in the days of Charlemagne, the Slavs stood on the Elbe and the Böhmerwald. A thousand years of European history had been rolled back."

Aside from these gloomy results, Potsdam was enlivened by two events: the news of the bomb and the American proposition in regard to the world's waterways.

On the first day of the conference, Mr. Stimson, the American Secretary of War, called on Sir Winston Churchill and showed him a piece of paper on which was written, "Babies satisfactorily born." This meant that the experiment in the New Mexican desert had succeeded. The new age had begun. "This dire quest," as Sir Winston describes the project, had made it possible for man, always the most destructive of God's creatures, to destroy everything.

To begin with, the bomb made it not only possible but easy to destroy Japan. According to Mr. Truman and Mr. Stimson and Sir Winston, there was never any question of refusing to use the bomb. It was regarded as "a merciful abridgment of the slaughter," and the word "merciful" is not to be taken cynically. "I thought immediately," writes Sir Winston, "of how the Japanese people, whose courage I had always admired, might find in the apparition of this almost supernatural weapon an excuse which would save their honour and release them from their obligation of being killed to the last fighting man."[4]

Less startling than the atomic bomb, but startling by normal standards, was Mr. Truman's proposal for the waterways of the world. The Russians, as they have done for centuries, were grumbling about the Black Sea straits and the fact that they had no unimpeded warm-water access to the oceans. This is a true grievance, and Mr. Truman proposed a true answer—very much to the distaste of the Russians. "I announced," he writes, "that . . . I was offering as a solution of the straits problem the suggestion that the Kiel Canal in Germany, the Rhine-Danube waterway from the North Sea to the Black Sea, the Black Sea straits, the Suez Canal, and the Panama Canal be made free waterways for the passage of freight and passengers of all countries, except for the fees for

4. We now know that members of the Japanese government expressed a willingness to discuss surrender four days before the first bomb was dropped. The President and his advisers have therefore been charged with cold-blooded indifference. But the suggestions of surrender were made behind the back of the military clique that dominated the Japanese cabinet. Even after Hiroshima and Nagasaki, these implacable men refused to accept peace until they were overruled by an imperial order and until their dying effort at a coup d'état had failed. Then, at last, the self-sufficient army in Manchuria bowed to the inevitable.

their necessary operation and maintenance." Elsewhere Mr. Truman describes this as "my proposal to join in an organization to free the waterways of the world" and adds that Sir Winston thought it a "remarkable and important" proposal. This indeed it was. Had the Russians agreed, the plan would have provided free access for the West to the heart of Communist-controlled eastern Europe. So the proposal was praised faintly and set to one side as politely as possible. Nothing good was to come out of Potsdam.

And nothing could ever be the same again after Potsdam. The old Europe was gone forever. The heir to the Western Roman Empire, which had for so long been the center of world power, disposing almost absent-mindedly of the destinies of far-away people, was now a center of weakness, the destiny of which was to be decided elsewhere. And the heir to the Eastern Roman Empire had come belatedly of age, had taken over a third of Europe almost by default, and was prepared to absorb the rest unless the United States and the British Commonwealth could build a coalition for resistance.

None of the old terms of reference made sense. None of the old short cuts in thinking could be relied upon. We went on using words like "France," "Germany," "Europe," as if we knew what they meant. But they had lost their former meanings, and we did not yet know what their new meanings would be. Nobody knew. Not even the wisest Frenchman, with his genius for definition, could tell you what

"France" meant in 1945. Yet Russia and the United States seemed fated to struggle for the soul and for the future hopes and opportunities of this indefinable place.

And, to add to the confusion, in the background of all men's minds at Potsdam (assuming, as seems reasonable, that the Russians had known about the "secret" from the beginning) was the bomb. Not only was the old Europe gone—changed from the subject, which acts, into the object, which is acted upon—but war itself, the final assertion of power, seemed to have lost its time-honored meaning. For if war had come to mean annihilation, how could it be a method for imposing a policy?

The Western leaders at Potsdam may have been as carefree as they say they were over the decision to use the atom bomb upon Japan, to finish the war while the bomb was still a monopoly. But, peering into the future, when many nations would possess this hateful device, they must have felt rather like the Earl of Douglas in the ballad:

> But I hae dreamed a dreary dream
> Beyond the Isle o' Skye,
> I saw a dead man win a fight,
> And I think that man was I.

II

1946: The Year of Frustration

1

In 1946 Dean Acheson remarked that Americans have an odd name for problems. "We call them headaches," he said; "you take a powder and they are gone." Then he warned that the stately "headaches" of the postwar years would not dissolve before pills or powders. "We have got to understand that all our lives the danger, the uncertainty, the need for alertness, for effort, for discipline will be upon us. It will be hard for us."

If anyone wonders why such a useful and intelligent man as Mr. Acheson became the center of intense hatred, the symbol for most of our troubles, a partial answer lies in those few sentences. He knew, unpopularly soon, that America had exchanged comfort for inquietude and safety for danger and that there was no turning back. Being one of the first to call attention to these facts, he was blamed for not altering the course of history instead of being thanked for predicting it. People attacked him for his clothes, his accent, and even his mustache, but the real trouble was his brain. Cassandra, after all, was not hated because she was good-looking or well dressed or because her family was important. She was hated because she told the truth. (And perhaps she, too, told it *de haut en bas*, which makes the truth even more distressing than usual.)

The year 1946 was enough to make anybody resent the moral lesson stated by Mr. Acheson. It was a year that offered all the frustrations of reconversion at home and of continued danger abroad. There were shortages in most consumer goods; there were large-scale strikes that inconvenienced everyone; and there was the discovery by millions of soldiers that they were not in fact returning to the dream-country with which they had comforted themselves during their loneliness abroad. There had probably never been a war fought more matter-of-factly, for the simple purpose of ending it. The chief war aim was to get home; and, since the quickest way to do that was to beat the enemy, everyone was in favor of beating him. The men were discouraged, therefore, and in many cases angry, when they found how much "home" had changed while their backs were turned.

And it had changed for exactly the reasons that Dean Acheson mentioned: our problems were no longer headaches to be dispersed by the proper treatment, they were roadblocks created by centuries of history. We could neither charge through them with our old impatience nor blast them out of the way with our new bombs. We had to sit down quietly and consider how, if at all, they could be circumvented. But this was not the average soldier's view of America: a nation beset by problems that perhaps could never be solved. "The Germans are beaten, aren't they? The Japanese are beaten? So what's all the trouble about?" And then came the not unnatural question, "Who has been selling us out while we were away?"

The strikes, luckily, were a problem that could be solved, in spite of much bitterness and some discomfort. There was enough to go round, and it was chiefly the general mood of discontent that imbued the strikers with so much anger. In the case of a threatened railway strike, which would have stopped every train in the country, the settlement did not come until Mr. Truman was standing before Congress, asking for a law that would allow him to draft strikers into the armed forces, on the ground that the government had temporarily seized the railways in order to keep them running and that the men were striking against the United States. This would have been a dangerous and probably an unconstitutional measure. The fact that Mr. Truman, a friend of labor, should ask for such a law is a sign of the fear that was in the air. Even Senator Taft—who, when not exacerbated by the sight of foreigners, was a humane man—found this proposal shocking.

1946: The Year of Frustration

2

While the strikes and the shortages were a steady nuisance at home, the major troubles of 1946 were still Russia and the bomb. The conference at Potsdam had set up a Council of Foreign Ministers to draft treaties with the satellite countries and with Italy. The first two meetings were held in London in September and in Moscow in December, 1945. The results were negligible. The third meeting was at Paris. Senator Vandenberg accompanied Secretary of State James F. Byrnes as consultant. The council met, off and on, from April until October. The purpose was a peace treaty with Italy and, incidentally, with Hungary, Rumania, Bulgaria, and Finland. Nothing was accomplished; but the difficulties in the way of all future agreements are made clear in Senator Vandenberg's notes. The Senator had planned to be "firm, but patient." He found the first task easier than the second—and doubtless his Russian opposite numbers felt the same way. Here are some of the Senator's *cris de cœur:*

"May 1, 1946. . . . The shadow-boxing is about over. There is no sense in carrying on this Punch-and-Judy business. . . . If it is humanly possible, through scrupulous fair play to Russia and by a super-generous attitude toward her legitimate needs, to bind up a working agreement with the Russkies, this *must* be done. But if the only price is our 'unconditional surrender,' it is best to find it out before too late. . . . The tragedy of it all is that the rest of this sick world could agree on a total post-war program in twenty minutes.

"May 2, 1946. . . . This can't go on much longer. I confess that I admire the way Molotov argues tenaciously for his positions. But the trouble is they have had so much from us for so long that they have not yet sensed the fact that our 'surrender days' are over."

On May 6 the Senator noted that even Mr. Ernest Bevin, the Socialist British foreign secretary, who had once hoped that "Left could speak to Left," found himself as frustrated as the rest of them. "If I can be given credit for an honest motive for a moment . . . ," he once burst out to Molotov. And a few minutes later, "Now that you've got *that* off your chest, Mr. Molotov, I hope you feel better." Unhappily, we don't know what the Russians were thinking. But we can guess that they, too, felt thwarted. Eight years after that Paris conference, when both the United States and Russia had developed "useful" H-bombs, President Eisenhower said: "We have arrived at the point . . . [where] there is just no real alternative to peace." If that should be true—and it is surely an optimistic statement—there is also no alternative to our understanding at least some small part of the Russian case and to admitting that we too, seen from the banks of the Volga, may look a bit odd. For we shall almost certainly fight, whatever happens to the human race or to the earth itself, if the two nations continue to see each other as inexplicable and therefore malign. Man is good at dying and, on the whole, finds it a more restful task than thinking—especially thinking in terms that deny his customary values.

In spite of all the ancient ambitions of a continental empire in their blood streams and all the new intolerance of communism on the surface of their minds, the Russians doubtless spend most of each week in thinking about their food, their drink, their love affairs, their salaries, and whether there is any purpose in man's life other than larding the lean earth when he dies. Throughout this book the Russians will seem rude and grasping. Sometimes they will seem stupid from the point of view of their own interests. But let us remember that we have no access to their documents and that at the moment they do not seem to be producing poetry. Without one or the other (preferably both) and without even visiting their land, we cannot hope to understand. So we must resist their encroachments, "frustrate their knavish tricks," and try not to get overexcited. No wonder it has been a difficult decade. Yet the best we can expect is another one just as difficult, since the alternative is a nice clean planet with no people on it.

3

While the foreign ministers were failing to agree on treaties in Paris, a United Nations commission in New York was failing to agree on the control of atomic energy and of the bomb. Here was the most perplexing and the most hate-creating of all America's troubles with Russia. We—the people and the administration alike—felt a grievous responsibility for the bomb. We wanted to do what was right. We put forward a plan that we thought magnanimous. The Russians treated it not only impolitely but disdainfully. From that day to this, the wound has remained open and uncomfortable.

Soon after the first atomic bombs were used upon Japan, Senator Vandenberg wrote: "I am sure of just one thing—namely, that the blackout curtain of secrecy must be lifted from every quarter of the globe before *anything* can be done in respect to a constructive program."

Shortly before the first meeting of the United Nations Commission on Atomic Energy, tests were held by the American Navy at Bikini (on July 1, 1946). The tests were for strategic purposes only. The more advanced types of bombs, said Mr. Truman, were already on hand but had not yet been tried. Yet even the old-fashioned bombs, a few months out of date, had an uncanny effect on the first Americans who were allowed to take a close look at the results. According to Mr. Desmond Young: "When American sailors went aboard the survived target ships at Bikini, they gradually became gripped by a strange, obsessive fear. 'Decks you can't stay on for more than a few minutes; air you can't breathe without a gas-mask but which smells like all other air; water you can't swim in; fish you can't eat; it's a fouled-up world,' they said."

There are the two chief evils of our time: "the blackout curtain of secrecy," which makes us afraid of our neighbors, and the miasma of "a fouled-up world." We owe them both to the physicists.

A fortnight after those tests at Bikini, we presented our plan to the United Nations commission. Perhaps the timing was wrong. Perhaps a few less inedible fish in the Pacific might have helped us to get a better hearing. Yet the plan would have put an end both to secrecy and to any further poisoning of the earth's surface. It provided for an International Atomic Development Authority, to which the United States would turn over its atomic secrets, provided that there were international control and inspection. The control and inspection were to apply to all nations and to be subject to no veto. Further manufacture of bombs was to cease immediately, and existing bombs were to be destroyed.

From that day to this, most Americans have believed that the Russian refusal to take this proposal seriously was one of the major calamities in history. The counterproposal—that atomic weapons should be outlawed but that there should be no international control or inspection—seemed silly without being funny. Nobody could be expected to agree; yet, if anyone laughed, he increased the deadly tension. Secrecy was now assured; the hateful and inaccurate word "security" was now to poison not only our languages but our lives. And, worst of all, the men of science, no longer permitted to live freely in the world-wide fraternity of scholars, would become less efficient or more "traitorous" or both.

The Russians, one must suppose, thought the West would

interfere with their domestic affairs if they permitted international control and inspection of developments in the field of atomic power. The Americans, we know, thought the Russians would cheat if we agreed to outlaw atomic weapons without international inspection. So, instead of an International Atomic Development Authority—under whose auspices we might have dared to dream that

> The world's great age begins anew,
> The golden years return—

we created the United States Atomic Energy Commission, under whose auspices even the brief war-fostered trust in our allies has quickly (and inevitably) been suppressed. The first report of the advisory committee to this commission, signed by two of the prime wizards who have made our sad new world—Enrico Fermi and J. R. Oppenheimer—ends with the following warning: "We have been forced to recognize, in studying the possible implementation of technical policy, how adverse the effect of secrecy, and of the inevitable misunderstanding and error which accompany it, have been on progress. . . . Even in the fields of technology, in industrial application . . . the fruits of secrecy are misapprehension, ignorance and apathy. It will be a continuing problem for the Government of the United States to re-evaluate the risks of unwise disclosure, and weigh them against the undoubted dangers of maintaining secrecy at the cost of error and stagnation."

A "provocative" letter, wrote Mr. Truman, and then added

his own decision, from which there was no appeal, on the question of secrecy: "I have been uncompromisingly opposed to sharing or yielding atomic military secrets to any other government." Thus began the dreary round of broken promises and of broken hopes for increased good will among the late allies. And thus began the feeling of conspiracy: spies, counterspies, fear of foreigners, fear of "subversive" types at home, fear of the next-door neighbor, and, finally, the use of the phrase "security risk" to describe a man who in peacetime refuses to allow congressmen to decide what he may talk about in public.

Most of us are scarcely aware of this last indignity, because most of us are far too ignorant to talk about anything that could interest a modern spy. Only a higher mathematician can hope to be hounded by beautiful females today. Yet even a higher mathematician is heir to the creative centuries during which Western man fought for the right to say what he thinks—at least when his country is alleged to be at peace. But the Russians abolished the old idea of peace when they refused an International Atomic Authority, and we accepted the abolition when we said that, in view of their refusal, secrecy must prevail. Perhaps it must. We are a long way from knowing the end of that story. Perhaps, on the other hand, we shall discover that we cannot afford those fruits of secrecy: "misapprehension, ignorance, and apathy." And in the meantime let us learn from Russian history since its earliest czarist days that true secrecy, efficient secrecy, is expensive: darkness at home and a minimum of mingling with foreign devils abroad.

If this is indeed the price we agreed to pay in the hope of keeping one jump ahead of the Russians, let us greet the apotheosis of "security" in the words of Alexander Pope:

> Lo! thy dread empire, Chaos! is restor'd;
> Light dies before thy uncreating word:
> Thy hand, great Anarch! lets the curtain fall;
> And universal Darkness buries all.

4

Meanwhile, in the midst of these unreassuring events and in spite of long-drawn-out wrangles before the United Nations about Russian troops in Iran, the United States diminished her armed forces from about eleven million men to about one million. But the President and his advisers, although powerless to resist the demand for demobilization, were becoming more and more wary, more and more hopeless about ever seeing the rosy world that had been envisaged by Franklin Roosevelt and Harry Hopkins at Yalta. Mr. Byrnes declared, apropos of Iran, that the United States would not "stand aloof if force or the threat of force is used contrary to the purposes and principles" of the Charter of the United Nations. He did not say what we would refuse to "stand aloof" with; but in case it was the atom bomb, the Persians might well have shuddered at the thought of our help.

Mr. Truman put the change in the official mood succinctly.

1946: The Year of Frustration

"Churchill had tried to get me not to withdraw our troops from Prague," he said, referring to the pressures of April and May, 1945. "I told him we were bound to do that by our agreement with the Russians. But if I had known then what I know now, I would have ordered the troops to go to the western boundaries of Russia."

It was perhaps in this temper of mind that he sponsored Sir Winston's speech in Fulton, Missouri, in March, 1946. The world was surprised by the frankness with which Sir Winston, in the heart of the isolationist Missouri Valley, named the Russian danger and called for an Anglo-American alliance to halt the "expansive tendencies" of the Soviet. But the President was not surprised. He had passed through and outlived his own stage of thinking that the former Prime Minister was merely an old-fashioned imperialist who fretted unnecessarily about the "Eastern question." Yet he may well have been astonished by the severity with which the American public and a large part of the British public adhered in 1946 to the Truman views of 1945. Astonished or not, he met the widespread and bitter attacks on Sir Winston's speech with his customary refusal to retreat. "I knew what he was going to say. . . . I didn't care what he said. We pretend to believe in free speech, don't we?"

"What he said," of course, was what he had already said so often to Mr. Truman in eloquent cables, many of which were, in effect, first drafts of the Fulton speech. "From Stettin in the Baltic to Trieste in the Adriatic," he told the un-prepared Missourians, "an iron curtain has descended across the Continent. . . . I do not believe that Soviet Russia desires war. What they desire is the fruits of war and the indefinite expansion of their power and doctrines. . . . I am convinced that there is nothing they admire so much as strength, and there is nothing for which they have less respect than weak-ness, especially military weakness."

Was not that a dainty dish to set before the king? King Demos, in Britain and in America, had persuaded himself that the war was "over," that duty was done, and that further talk about military strength or weakness was "stirring up trouble." The millions of young Americans who had been demobilized during the previous ten months did not thank Sir Winston Churchill for that speech.

Today, unhappily, it is the fashion to forget what Ameri-cans thought or hoped about Russia in 1946. Any politician who is willing to be reminded of the truth should re-read the impolite distaste with which the press greeted Sir Winston's moderate comments. Alternatively, he might re-read Mr. Henry Wallace's speech of September, 1946, which proved to be alarmingly close to the temper of the day. True, Mr. Wallace lost his job because of the speech, but that was be-cause the mood of the Administration had changed, not be-cause the public was outraged.

In spite of the fact that Roosevelt had pushed him out of

1946: The Year of Frustration

the vice-presidency in favor of Mr. Truman, Henry Wallace thought himself the true heir of the Roosevelt tradition and of the New Deal. According to that tradition, Russia was a friendly nation that would respond to kindness and that would be deeply wounded by such remarks as Sir Winston's. So Mr. Wallace, although he was Secretary of Commerce, attacked the entire foreign policy of the Truman Administration. He insisted that the policy meant getting needlessly "tough" with Russia. And he also attacked Sir Winston's idea of an alliance between Britain and America, which he said would lead to war. "I am neither anti-British nor pro-British," he said, "neither anti-Russian nor pro-Russian." Then he added the sentence that made the speech into an international incident of some consequence: "And just two days ago, when President Truman read these words, he said that they represented the policy of his Administration."

This was on September 12. Mr. Byrnes, the American Secretary of State, was in Paris, trying to negotiate with the Russians for at least one treaty of peace that might bring hope to at least one half-ruined country somewhere in Europe. Senator Vandenberg was with him, officially as consultant but in fact as the only man who could answer "Yes" or "No" for the Republican party in the Senate. When the text of Wallace's ill-omened speech reached Paris, the press of all the world besieged the angry Secretary and the discouraged Senator. What did this mean? Were they both now in disgrace? Was the Secretary of Commerce to become Secretary of State?

Very few people in Europe or Asia understand that a member of the Cabinet in the United States is merely an administrative assistant, hired by the President (with the consent of the Senate) to supervise one small section of the President's onerous job, but with no power to make policy, no political responsibility, and subject to dismissal (with nobody's consent and no repercussions) whenever the President is tired of his face. The British parliamentary system is the model that most Europeans and Asiatics have vaguely in mind whenever they think about "democracy." Under the parliamentary system, Mr. Wallace's speech was tantamount to a palace revolution in Turkey: heads must roll. A head did roll in this case, but only because of the sentence in which the President was alleged to have agreed with what his own Cabinet member was saying.

Vandenberg promptly issued a statement to the French press, to the effect that, while most Republicans were in favor of a bipartisan foreign policy, "we can only cooperate with one Secretary of State at a time." Mr. Byrnes was rather more blunt and rather more bitter. "The world today is in doubt not only as to American foreign policy, but as to *your* foreign policy," he told the President. "You and I spent fifteen months building a bipartisan policy. We did a fine job convincing the world that it was a permanent policy upon which the world could rely. Wallace destroyed that in a day."

1946: The Year of Frustration

Vandenberg and Byrnes seem to have assumed as a matter of course that Henry Wallace was romancing when he said that "President Truman read these words" and had agreed that they were the policy of the government of the United States. The extraordinary fact is that nobody knows to this day whether Mr. Wallace was mistaken or not. Within the last few months he has reaffirmed that he and the President went over the speech together, page by page, before it was delivered. And Mr. Truman still asserts that nothing of the sort ever happened. Since one of them must be flatly wrong, we can only wish we had more documents. In any case, in the words of Mr. Clark Clifford, counsel to the President: "Wallace spoke, and hell broke loose next morning. Oh, boy, it really did!"

Every effort to diminish the "hell" made it slightly worse, since both Mr. Truman and Mr. Wallace seemed convinced that the other was prevaricating. Mr. Wallace lost his job on September 20, eight days after the speech. So far as the outside world was concerned, that was the answer; the crisis was over. The foreign offices thought that they knew, once again, where America stood. But at home the affair could not be so easily forgotten. What on earth was happening, if the President could not even remember whether he approved or disapproved of a startling statement by a member of his official family? The thing became a symbol for the year of discontent, the "Year of Frustration," as the press had begun to call it.

Americans are impatient, and 1946 was no year for impatient people. The controversy over the Wallace speech and the crossed purposes that the controversy revealed became the focus for a wide unrest. This was unlucky for Mr. Truman and for the Democratic party. Eight weeks after the speech came the mid-term elections, the first public challenge to the brave little man who had hurried so unsuspectingly to the White House on April 12, 1945.

The Republican party, which had not elected a President since 1928 or a majority in either House of Congress since 1930, found the perfect slogan for this year of discontent: "Had Enough?" The billboards were plastered with those simple words. The most bumbling chairman, using the phrase at the most inappropriate moment in a much-too-long speech, would be startled by the applause. Massachusetts might argue with Iowa about the ingredients of the indigestible surfeit, but all wished for a change of diet. In the new House of Representatives, the Republicans had 246 members and the Democrats 188. There were 51 Republicans in the new Senate (where only a third of the members come up for election at any one time), and 45 Democrats.[1]

1. Before the election the figures for the House were 243 Democrats and 190 Republicans, and for the Senate, 57 Democrats and 38 Republicans.

III

The Eightieth Congress

The new Republican Congress, which met for its first session in January, 1947, was an unlucky assembly. It was no worse than most congresses, in brains and experience, but it seemed worse, because so much was expected of it in domestic affairs, where it could do next to nothing, and so little credit was awarded it in foreign affairs, where it did supremely well.

The Republicans officially disapproved of almost everything that had happened since 1933—except victory in the war. And even victory was tarnished with insecurity and worry by the end of 1946. The millions who had "had enough" longed for a return to a vanished America. This was hard to arrange.

The new Congress could lower taxes gently, but, in doing so, it gave the Democrats a talking point for 1948: the reductions favored the rich. And the new Congress could pass a labor-management relations bill (the Taft-Hartley Act) that inadvertently handed the President millions of votes.

These bills were neither so wicked nor so class-conscious as the Democrats pretended, but, on the other hand, they failed conspicuously to promote the Republican dream of restoring 1928. At that date, for example, labor had no sanction for its right to organize; but the much-abused Taft-Hartley Act of 1947, while banning the "closed shop," indorsed the "union shop" (which requires a worker to toe the line *after* he accepts his job). This is still a far cry from the "good old days."[1]

Almost the only thing that Congress could do consistently to satisfy the Republican voters was to refuse to enact the reforms that Mr. Truman requested. It could not undo the New Deal, but it could prevent further changes. Yet here, too, it played into the hands of the President, who had only to ask

1. The original act permitted the "union shop" only if the union represented a majority of those eligible to vote in a collective bargaining election. This restriction was repealed in October, 1951. The other major features of the act are: (1) it permits employers to sue unions for broken contracts or damages inflicted during strikes; (2) it requires unions to abide by a 60-day "cooling-off period" before striking; (3) it requires unions to make public their financial statements; (4) it forbids union contributions to political campaigns; (5) it forbids the "check-off system" under which the employer collects union dues; (6) it requires union leaders to take an oath that they are not members of the Communist party. (The last point was challenged at law and upheld by the Supreme Court in 1950, Justice Black dissenting.) Whether these are wise or acceptable provisions, time will show. But they must have been reasonably popular provisions in June, 1947. The House passed the act by a vote of 320 to 70 (217 Republicans and 103 Democrats voting with the majority), and the Senate approved it by 54 to 17 (37 Republicans and 17 Democrats in favor). When it came to overriding the President's veto, the vote was larger in both Houses, but the proportion for and against was about the same.

and ask again for a long list of popular and expensive measures, such as extended social security and federal aid to education. He could make his requests as idealistic and as far-reaching as he chose, for he knew that they would be refused and that he could then put the blame upon the Republicans—even if there was every likelihood that his own party would have refused the same requests. Thus he built the legend of the Eightieth Congress—the "Do-Nothing Congress," the "worst Congress in history"—which stood him in such good stead in 1948.

The man who best symbolized the mood of this Eightieth Congress in domestic matters was Senator Robert A. Taft of Ohio. The son of a President of the United States, he had entered the Senate in 1939 at the age of fifty. He quickly became the most influential member of the opposition. Tall, rumpled, with a middle western twang and a broad grin that could express distaste almost as readily as pleasure, his character and his knowledge made him a natural leader. He was conservative in his thinking as well as in his manners and taste, and he was an extreme nationalist—a word that he preferred to "isolationist." His instinctive response to American commitments abroad was that they should be diminished, and to social legislation at home that it should be rejected. Even the wisest laws, he felt, could, at best, prevent evil rather than promote good. He was intolerant of the complaining voter and of the ignorant politician. When asked what people should do about the soaring meat prices after the war, he answered, "Eat less." And one of his favorite comments on the speeches of other senators was, "That's stupid."

Such a man most properly became the hero of all who mourned an earlier, simpler, more forthright America, more sure of its values and, above all, more self-contained than the perplexed America of the postwar years. And yet his impatience with fools, his tactlessness and stiffness, perhaps even his extreme partisanship, kept him at four successive conventions from receiving his party's nomination for the presidency. He became the symbol of the party's desires; he was nationally known as "Mr. Republican"; he was worshiped by the right wing; but at the last moment the conventions always gave the prize to another man: Wendell Willkie, Governor Dewey, General Eisenhower.

The year 1947, however, should have been his golden hour. When the newly elected legislature assembled, the press called it "Taft's Congress"; he was expected to dominate it easily. But as he himself said: "It would be ironical if this Congress which really has its heart set on straightening out domestic affairs would end up in being besieged by foreign problems." Woodrow Wilson made a similar remark when he came to the presidency in 1913, knowing nothing about foreign affairs and hoping to be allowed to maintain his innocence. Wilson was soon doing his best to learn about the irritating inhabitants of other countries. Taft never even tried.

The Eightieth Congress

But luckily there was another Republican senator, less representative of the nostalgic dreams of the party, more aware of the irrelevance of such dreams, who could lead the Eightieth Congress in facing the heavy decisions that were thrust upon it.

"Without the inspired self-reversal and the brilliant, intelligent leadership of Senator Arthur Vandenberg," writes Mr. Truman, "and that of Charles A. Eaton, chairman of the House Foreign Affairs Committee, we could never have achieved any by-partisan policy in the conduct of foreign affairs. Without the leadership of these enlightened Republicans, during those two years, the United Nations, the Marshall Plan, NATO, and other projects would have been hampered, if not blocked completely, by the selfish Republican majority." The tribute seems a little churlish. After all, the "inspired" leadership was provided by Republicans. And a Republican majority, whether selfish or not, supported all the brave decisions of the next two years. And Mr. Truman's future reputation will largely rest upon these decisions.

Oddly enough, the Republicans themselves have rarely claimed the credit that Mr. Truman here denies them. They were so chagrined at being unable to "straighten out domestic affairs"—i.e., undo the works of Franklin Roosevelt—that they seemed ashamed to call attention to the wisdom and the sense of responsibility that they had displayed abroad. This unusual shyness, plus Mr. Truman's savage attacks during the campaign of 1948, largely explains the malodor of the "Do-Nothing Congress," which might just as appropriately have been known as the "Decisive Congress."

In January, 1947, Mr. Byrnes resigned as Secretary of State and was succeeded by General George C. Marshall. Like Henry Wallace, James Byrnes had expected to be nominated to the vice-presidency in 1944. Both men felt that they had more right to be in the White House than the man who actually was there, and neither had served the new President wholeheartedly. The relationship was awkward both ways. "I don't know how I ever got out of that mudhole," said Mr. Truman, referring to the Cabinet and the advisers he had inherited from Roosevelt. But now, with General Marshall, he had the man beside him whom he admired most, and the change came just in time.

In February, 1947, the British government informed the Department of State that, for reasons of finance and of manpower, the United Kingdom must withdraw all support to Greece by March 30. The Greek economy, the note pointed out, was on the point of collapse; if no one took up the burden that the British were forced to lay down, Greece would presumably have a Communist revolution. Turkey's independence would then be impossible to defend, and, with the loss of Turkey, the whole of the Middle East might become, like eastern Europe, a satellite to Moscow. This was unwelcome news—doubly unwelcome because American liberals had been harshly critical of the British for holding the fort in Greece. How was Mr. Truman to explain that an allegedly wicked example of British imperialism was now to become the policy—the dangerous and expensive policy—of the United States? Senator Vandenberg gave him the answer: "Mr. President," he said at the end of a conference at the White House, "if that's what you want, there's only one way to get it. That is to make a personal appearance before Congress and scare hell out of the country."

Nobody was more averse than Vandenberg to what he called "crisis diplomacy." He repeatedly criticized President Roosevelt and President Truman for allowing affairs to drift until something had to be done in a mad hurry, until even a second-best decision was better than no decision at all. But this time he saw that the hurry was not the fault of the Administration. "We confront a condition and not a theory," he admitted, and he rose magnificently to defend the President's efforts.

On March 12, the President went before a joint session of Congress and asked for $400,000,000 for military and economic aid to the Greek and Turkish governments, and he asked for authorization to send Americans to advise and guide in the use of the aid. "I believe," he said, "that it must be the policy of the United States to support free peoples who are resisting attempted subjugation by armed minorities or by outside pressures." This is the "Truman Doctrine," the basis of American foreign policy from that day forth. "The President's message faces the facts," said Vandenberg, "and so must Congress." And so did Congress, to its great honor, in spite of attacks from the anti-imperialist left and from the economy-minded right, which, as usual, predicted bankruptcy.

While Washington was accepting this large involvement in the defense of free people, western Europe seemed to be going downhill fast. In May, 1947, Sir Winston Churchill said: "What is Europe now? It is a rubble-heap, a charnel house, a breeding-ground of pestilence and hate." In slightly more gentle language the Department of State had been sending similar reports to itself all winter. And under the prodding of General Marshall and of the President, the department and its advisers had been studying one of the most disquieting questions ever to face a government: Could Europe be saved? The time had passed for small gestures of help: food here, a loan there, a technical mission somewhere else. In spite of such well-meant efforts, Europe remained a rubble-heap. Even Britain seemed not far from economic collapse during that ugly spring.

So General Marshall created a Policy Planning Staff in the Department of State, under Mr. George Kennan, and told it to report on whether there was anything we could do, no matter how enormous the effort, to stave off ruin. Mr. Kennan was a fortunate choice. Unlike many American diplomats, he had never thought the world could be remade as we should like to see it; he had merely hoped it might be prevented from going irrevocably wrong. Also, he had had long experience in Russia.

The first sign that the Administration believed that it was not yet too late, that Europe was not yet lost, came from Dean Acheson, Undersecretary of State, in a speech at a small college in Mississippi. He reaffirmed the Truman Doctrine emphatically, and added: "Since world demand exceeds our ability to supply, we are going to have to concentrate our emergency assistance in areas where it will be most effective in building world political and economic stability." The words may sound innocent, but behind them lay a decision that was to divide the American people more bitterly than any other modern issue and to cause seemingly sane men to listen with approval when General Marshall was called a traitor. The decision was to concentrate our major efforts on helping the recovery of western Europe rather than on helping Chiang Kai-shek win his civil war in China.

Not only was Chiang thought incapable of attracting enough support to build a nation, even if we supplied him with a brief victory, but the loss of China (with its poverty in iron, oil, and industry) was not regarded as a major threat to the United States, whereas the loss of western Europe might prove fatal. And Europe, the Administration thought, could save herself permanently with our help, while Chiang

73

The Price of Power

could not. So the President, faced with the fact that "world demand exceeds our ability to supply," chose to supply the West. The way was now clear for the Marshall Plan and for the subsequent frenzy of those to whom the Pacific is the Republican ocean.

On June 5, 1947, General Marshall spoke at Harvard University. "It is already evident," he said, "that before the United States Government can proceed much further . . . there must be some agreement among the countries of Europe as to the requirements of the situation and the part those countries themselves will take. . . . The initiative, I think, must come from Europe. . . . The Program should be a joint one, agreed to by a number, if not all, of the European nations."

This was a strange proposal to lay before the country during the first six months of "Taft's Congress," which was dedicated to lowering taxes and cutting government expenditure. Senators muttered; but in London Foreign Secretary Ernest Bevin said, "This is the turning-point." Within three weeks the British and French governments had called all Europe to Paris to discuss the idea.

Russia might have smothered the plan at birth by taking part enthusiastically and asking—for her satellites if not for herself—aid on a scale that America must refuse. But Russia said "No." And she ordered Poland and Czechoslovakia to change their eager "Yes" into a reluctant "No." Here, as later, she did her best to make the Marshall Plan seem wise and statesman-like to the American people.

The Eightieth Congress

Sixteen nations that were not subject to Russia's "No" met throughout the summer, set their own industrial and agricultural targets, made vague propitiatory gestures toward the removal of trade and monetary barriers, and presented the United States with a four-year plan for economic rehabilitation that would require $17,000,000,000 of American assistance.[2]

Meanwhile, at home, the Administration was inquiring into what the American people could afford to contribute, and Vandenberg was preparing for one of the great battles in the history of the Senate. "Evidently I am to have some degree of trouble with Bob Taft," he wrote his wife in November, 1947. "So be it! The world is full of tragedy; but there is no tragedy greater than that we have to have a presidential election next year in the U.S.A. That must be what's biting Robert."

Not only was "Robert" on the extreme right giving trouble (on the usual grounds that no good could come of helping foreigners and that in any case this meant bankruptcy), but so was Henry Wallace on the left. To him, this was a wanton attack on the Soviet Union, a provocation to war, a "Martial Plan."

Such was the atmosphere in January, 1948, when the debate began in earnest. Assaulted by sullen growls from the con-

2. The first figure, which was luckily reduced, had been $29,000,000,000. A little over $13,000,000,000 did the job. But between 1946 and 1955 the United States spent $51,000,000,000 on foreign aid of all types, western Europe receiving $33,400,000,000. According to President Eisenhower, this was a most wise investment, which realized a high rate of return.

servatives and by shrill screams from the liberals, the Administration might have surrendered except for Vandenberg. He would allow no hurry, for he knew that the country—as it argued in every parlor, club, church, town hall, and bar— was coming to his side. And he would allow no factious bitterness. Whenever his opponents made a wise point, he would suggest a wise concession—so long as it did not infringe on the purpose of the bill. He agreed, for example (and he persuaded the President and General Marshall to agree) that, since no Congress can bind its successor in regard to spending and since the sum of $17,000,000,000 was "only an educated guess" as to what might be needed, the Administration should accept $5,000,000,000 for the first year plus a recommendation that the program should go forward. He agreed that the plan should be administered by an independent agency, not by the Department of State. And he agreed to write into the act the following sentence: "The continuity of assistance provided by the United States should at all times be dependent upon the continuity of co-operation among the countries involved."

These are the salutary "concessions" which concede nothing vital but which win votes. In February, the Foreign Relations Committee approved the bill by a vote of 13 to nothing. On March 1, Vandenberg defended it on the floor of the Senate. He had already won his fight—even Taft admitted he would vote for the bill—but he was now intent upon the largest possible majority, so that Europe might have the largest possible confidence.

Vandenberg was not an orator, but he was a very careful speaker, who labored for weeks to make sure he was covering every useful point. And he knew the Senate as he knew his own family, so he could answer in advance the objections that every important member might be expected to raise. He began his speech on March 1 by asking for a prompt acceptance of his Economic Cooperation Act "in the name of peace, stability, and freedom."

The Russians, as usual, had done their best for the Marshall Plan: on February 25 they had suppressed the last remnants of freedom in Czechoslovakia and had pulled that most distressful land peremptorily behind the Iron Curtain. Also, on the very day that Vandenberg spoke, news from northern Europe suggested that Finland was about to receive the same treatment. "We are entirely surrounded by risks," said the Senator. "I profoundly believe that the pending program is the best of these risks. I have no quarrel with those who disagree, because we are dealing with imponderables. But I am bound to say to those who disagree that they have not escaped to safety by rejecting or subverting this plan. They have simply fled to other risks, and I fear far greater ones."

In this reasonable tone he reviewed the hard work and the

77

hard thinking that had gone into the plan on both sides of the Atlantic. It would apply, he said, to 270,000,000 people in Europe. The governments of those people and our own experts believed that the plan would suffice and that western Europe could be saved. As Vandenberg ended, he received a standing ovation. In two weeks' time the bill had passed the Senate by a vote of 60 to 17. On April 3, having passed the House of Representatives, it was signed by the President. A later attempt to sabotage the plan by cutting the necessary appropriations was met by Vandenberg with one of the most emotional appeals ever made in the Senate, for the honor of the United States. Again he was successful.

The fate of the Marshall Plan, however, was not decided merely, or even mostly, on the floor of the Senate. It was decided by the American people. There has never been a better example of how public opinion, in a sprawling federal nation, can inform itself and bring pressure to bear, once it has been roused to make the effort of thinking. All over the country hundreds of committees came together to discuss the Marshall Plan: the nature of the need, the possibility of meeting it, the cost in money to one's self and one's neighbors, the effect upon the safety of the United States. Other committees were organized to oppose the plan. But those in favor were markedly in the majority, and Congress was treated to the unusual experience of receiving petitions from large groups of people (the citizens, not infrequently, of very poor regions) in favor of a bill that must involve raising their taxes.[3]

In view of the passions that were soon to be aroused, it seems curious that the opponents of the bill did not talk more about the needs of Chiang Kai-shek and of Asia in general. But the public had no inkling of the huge disaster that was about to overwhelm Chiang. And Vandenberg, with his usual canniness, had induced the President to recommend— in addition to the European funds—$463,000,000 of economic and military aid for China. This was in effect a bribe to the Asia First group, in order that the rescue of Europe might go forward. It was expensive, but it worked.

Even after the bill for the Marshall Plan was passed, Russia continued to do everything she could to make the trouble and expense seem worthwhile. In June she refused once again to agree with the other occupying powers on the administration of Berlin, and she insisted that Russian currency be used throughout the city. Britain, the United States, and France inaugurated their own currency reform in West Berlin. Thereupon, Russia blockaded all the land traffic routes between Berlin and the West—an intelligent and seemingly irresistible way of destroying British and American prestige in Germany.

---

3. *The Economist* (London) wrote: "Marshall Aid is the most straightforwardly generous thing that any country has ever done for others, the fullest expression so far of that American idealism on which all the hopes of the West depend."

As Mr. Truman said, if we moved out of Berlin, we would be risking everything which the Marshall Plan was intended to defend. Yet how could we stay, without daily danger of war with Russia? General Clay, our commander on the spot, told the President that we must stay, no matter what the cost. General Vandenberg of the United States Air Force told the President that if we tried, over any length of time, to supply the 2,100,000 residents of the blockaded region by air, we would seriously weaken our power to wage strategic warfare. Yet the President and the British government decided to go ahead with the airlift, since this seemed less dangerous than an attempt to push through armed road convoys. There was a chance that the Russians might not attack the airlift, especially if they felt sure it must fail.

General Clay said that by wintertime the minimum needed to keep Berlin alive without excessive hardship would be 4,500 tons a day. By October, the average was close to 5,000 tons a day, of which the British flew in about one-third. This extraordinary effort continued for 321 days, until May 12, 1949, when the Russians lifted the blockade on condition that the Council of Foreign Ministers reopen the entire German question. Meanwhile, at the height of the blockade, came the American presidential election.

2

Taft, as usual, had hoped for the Republican nomination, but the convention passed him over in favor of Governor

The Eightieth Congress

Thomas E. Dewey of New York. A number of Democrats wanted to get rid of Harry Truman, because, like everybody else (except Mr. Truman himself), they felt he was sure to be beaten. This anti-Truman group repeated the oldest pattern in the Democratic party: southern conservatives plus the bosses of the big "machines" in northern cities. Their one hope was General Eisenhower, whose politics were unknown but whose vote-getting powers were thought to be good.

Oddly enough, Mr. Truman himself had offered the job to General Eisenhower at Potsdam in 1945. "General," he said, "there is nothing you want that I won't try to help you get. That definitely and specifically includes the Presidency in 1948." The General laughed and refused the kind suggestion. He refused again, many times, during the preconvention months in 1948; but by that time the flattering promises of Democrats-for-Eisenhower were meaningless, because Mr. Truman had decided he wanted the job himself. And as he has said, "When the President is sitting in the White House, the national convention of his party has never gone against his recommendations in the choice of a candidate." So that was that.

The northern bosses groaned, not because of a distaste for Truman but because of a distaste for defeat. The southern conservatives did more than groan. They feared the President because of his steady efforts to secure first-class citizenship for the Negro. They formed a new party, which they called

The Price of Power

"States' Rights Democrats" ("Dixiecrats"), and nominated Mr. Strom Thurmond of South Carolina, who later won the electoral votes of four southern states. And meanwhile, in the North, the extreme left wing of the party—all those who thought the Administration had been needlessly impolite toward Russia—formed the "Progressive party" and nominated Henry Wallace, who got no electoral votes in November but who was popular enough in New York to deprive the Democrats of that important state.

So there was the little man again (or there he seemed to be), as on the day of Franklin Roosevelt's death: poor Harry Truman, in a predicament much too big for him. No one thought he had a chance even before his party split into three pieces. After the defection of Henry Wallace and the Dixiecrats, there seemed little use in bothering about a campaign. The newspapers, in terms of circulation, were 8 to 1 for Governor Dewey. The prophets and political seers were at least 99 to 1 for him. Mr. Elmo Roper stopped taking his polls, on the ground that it was a waste of time to ask questions when everyone knew the answers.

How did Mr. Truman do it? How did he win 304 electoral votes to 189 for Governor Dewey and 38 for Mr. Thurmond? There seem to have been three main reasons. One was Dewey's ill-advised campaign. It was patronizing from start to finish, and there can be no worse note to strike in politics; "God and the people hate a chesty man." Mr. Dewey pretended to be sad, rather than angry, about President Truman. Everyone, he suggested, knew the President's handicaps, and, after all, the whole sorry affair was merely an accident of death. These things have to happen from time to time. The country had been very patient with what he called "the Administration which happens to be in power at the moment." And now the patience would be rewarded—but apparently the Governor did not look so rewarding as all that, when the voters watched him tour the country on his "Victory Special."

We have already mentioned a second reason: the strange trap that the Republicans had dug for themselves in regard to the Eightieth Congress. Although that Congress had helped to save the world by the foreign policy which it had hammered out in collaboration with the Administration, the Republicans refrained from boasting about this rare accomplishment. Many of their voters, they seemed to feel, were not too keen on saving worlds; and in any case, how could they praise the foreign policy while looking down their noses with disdain at the Administration that had fathered it? At home, on the other hand, the record of the Congress was heaven-sent for Mr. Truman.

And Mr. Truman showed his warm gratitude to heaven. No gift has ever been put to better use, and this was the third and most important reason for success. He traveled thirty thousand miles. He made 315 set speeches and countless brief

The Price of Power

talks from the back platform at whistle stops. And he poured his scorn upon "that Republican Eightieth Congress, that do-nothing, good-for-nothing, worst Congress." It became a famous act, and if he seemed to be leaving it out, his audience would yell at him to "get going on Congress."

He not only "got going" on Congress; he put that unhappy legislature on show, so that the people could watch it doing nothing. On the night he accepted his nomination, he announced to the astonished convention that "on the twenty-sixth of July, which out in Missouri we called 'Turnip Day,' I am going to call Congress back and ask them to pass laws to halt rising prices and to meet the housing crisis—which they say they are for in their platform." Then he gave a long list of social legislation he would ask of Congress, each detail of which would appeal to some group of voters and the whole of which he knew Congress must reject. "They can do this job in fifteen days," he added, "if they want to do it. They still have time to go out and run for office."

It was crude politics, this special session which had either to lose Republican votes by doing what it was asked or lose independent votes by seeming to justify the name "Do-Nothing." But the public was more amused than shocked. Perhaps the crudity of the gesture was a relief from the supercilious airs of Mr. Dewey's entourage.

As the incredible night of November 2 wore on and the "certain" Republican victory began to seem more and more

84

The Eightieth Congress

unlikely, the most unexpected people were happy at seeing the experts look ridiculous. Even staunch Republicans rejoiced, for there is nothing more pleasing than the ancient ritual of the banana peel. The optimistic "Extra" of the *Chicago Tribune*, with its eight-column headline, "DEWEY DEFEATS TRUMAN," quickly became a collector's item.[4]

4. Mr. Truman received 24,045,052 votes, Mr. Dewey 21,896,927, Mr. Wallace 1,137,957, and Mr. Thurmond 1,168,687. There was also a Prohibition party and a Socialist party, but neither received 100,000 votes. The President received a large majority of the votes of labor and of the Negroes and a small majority of the farmers' votes. The votes in the Electoral College were, as usual, badly out of balance with the popular vote.

IV

Hiss, Chiang, Fuchs, and the Bomb

1

The President's triumph was fun. The American people enjoyed it. Our friends and enemies in Europe enjoyed it. And even in distant Asia—according to a traveler who spent that fabulous November night in Afghanistan—men and women heard that the proud had once more been humbled, and they laughed maliciously. But there was one unhappy aspect to an otherwise gay occasion: the Republican leaders and many important citizens throughout the land were not amused. They were angry and bewildered at this inexplicable defeat.

"I don't care how the thing is explained," said Senator Taft; "it defies all common sense." This can be a dangerous moment in a democracy, when proud men who think they belong by nature in the seats of power find themselves excluded once too often, and by an opponent for whom they have no respect. After all, between 1860 and 1928 the Republicans had won fourteen presidential elections and the Democrats four. It seemed clear to the average Republican businessman or lawyer or senator that he and his friends were intended to run the country. If something went disastrously wrong, the other chaps could take over for a few years and show their customary incompetence. This was the beauty of a two-party system: the Democrats were a safety valve against public indignation. But as soon as the temperature dropped, the safety valve should cease to function until the next near-explosion.

Then suddenly, in 1932, came the interminable Franklin Roosevelt. He won his first election in the conventional way: great depressions are expected to produce Democratic Presidents, and this one was at least a gentleman with a good Republican name. The election of 1936 was disappointing but not enraging. The other two Democrats to reach the White House since 1860 had each served two terms, so why should not this one? And then, by 1940, the world was inside out; the third term could be blamed on Hitler and other unreliable foreigners. Likewise the fourth term. But the election of 1948 came after three years of peace. Roosevelt the magician, the betrayer of his class, was dead. Harry Truman was nothing but an accident. The country could at last return to its natural allegiance, intrusting its future to the competent, experienced hands of the Grand Old Party.

When the whole of this agreeable dream-life collapsed,

when the country thumbed its nose at the Grand Old Party and chose the cocky little man from Missouri, the shock was inordinate to many thousand worthy, intelligent, and deeply patriotic families. In terms of the parents' generation, this was not unlike the disappointment that the soldiers had felt when they came home to a nation no longer safe and self-contained but caught forever in the whirlpool of world politics. In too many cases, both the parents and the children thought vaguely, irrationally, "Someone has been messing about with my America."

All that was needed was a demagogue to feed their fears and then to goad them with lying explanations. But first—to prepare for the villain's entrance—came Hiss, Chiang, Fuchs, and the Russian bomb.

2

Two months before Mr. Truman's pleasing but half-disquieting triumph, Whittaker Chambers accused Alger Hiss of having been a member of the Communist party between 1934 and 1938. This was not much of an accusation. In those depression-blighted years before Hitler gave all men employment—and long before the bomb—lots of Americans preened themselves in eccentric, provocative feathers. Some of them may have suffered from malnutrition while doing so, but at least they did not suffer from being told what to think.

If Hiss, when charged by Chambers before the House Un-American Activities Committee, had said, "Certainly I was a

Communist," this perverse, mischievous case might never have arisen. Hiss was no longer in the Department of State when Chambers attacked; he was head of the Carnegie Endowment for International Peace. In the first job it might have been awkward to have once belonged to an international conspiracy; in the second job it might almost have been an asset. And one can scarcely get overexcited about those ex-party members if one recalls the tedious wrangles at boring dinners in the 1930's, when lots of the silliest people alive thought it chic to be a Communist, so long as one was not a Trotskyite (whatever that might be). But, instead of saying nothing—or, better still, saying "Of course"—Hiss sued Chambers for $75,000. Thus he destroyed himself. He accepted the bizarre notion that it was shameful rather than ill-informed to have once believed in the Revolution. And he stirred the inscrutable Chambers into re-examining his memory and into finding a new charge that was truly discreditable.

Unhappily, before the second and more sinister act of the Chambers-Hiss drama, President Truman blundered onto the stage, falling over his own feet in the most approved clownish fashion but provoking no laughs at all. He was asked at a press conference what he thought of Chambers' accusation. He answered impatiently that all these investigations were merely a red herring, flaunted by the Eightieth Congress to distract people from noticing that it was doing nothing. When he won his own election on November 2—and especially when the chairman of the Un-American Activites Committee was indicted for malfeasance—Mr. Truman must have felt that his jibe had been an adequate answer. But he had left out of account the erratic, yet formidable, memory upon which Whittaker Chambers could draw.

In December, 1948, Chambers suddenly charged not only that Hiss had been a member of the party but that he had been a Communist spy while working in the Department of State and that he had copied classified documents which Chambers had then handed to the Russians. (Chambers, of course, was speaking as a spy of long standing whose sensitive conscience, now that he had once more changed sides, led him week by week to remember worse and worse things about his old associates.)

This time the President invited serious trouble and did himself and his country serious harm. Hiss was no longer charged nonsensically with having believed something that was fashionable when he believed it and hateful ten years later. He was charged with selling his country's secrets to a foreign power. And, even if the secrets were small ones that doubtless confused and bored the men in Moscow, this was a terrible charge against any citizen and doubly so if the citizen was in the service of his government. (And triply so, one might say, in the haunted world of atomic energy—though the unhappy Hiss could never have foreseen such a world when he was peddling his trivial bits and pieces.)

Hiss, Chiang, Fuchs, and the Bomb

Also, Chambers' new accusations were backed by a great deal of alleged evidence: classified documents said to have been copied in Hiss's handwriting, classified documents said to have been typed on Hiss's typewriter, and all of it illegally in the hands of this unclassified informer. The "evidence" had not yet been tested in court; yet it should not have been treated as a joke. Truman stuck to his story, however. He told a reporter the whole thing was still a red herring and that the Eightieth Congress was simply trying to sound as if it were serving a useful purpose. For this lightheartedness over a question that deeply perturbed the country, he has not been forgiven.

The excitement about the Hiss case was clearly inordinate. Even the second set of charges referred to events long before the war, at a time when most Americans would have been surprised to hear that we had "secrets" and might even have disapproved. Under the statute of limitations Hiss could not be indicted for espionage during those far-off days. But he could be indicted for perjury, for saying under oath that he had not passed restricted documents to Chambers and that he had not even seen Chambers since the end of 1936. This indictment the grand jury decided to bring, on December 15, 1948. The first trial began in the following May, but the jury could not agree. The second trial began in November, and Hiss was found guilty.

Long before the verdict, most people had firm convictions

as to Hiss's guilt or innocence. The convictions were held with a passion that transcended the interesting but tenuous evidence. And among those who were confident of innocence, few seemed to change their minds after the adverse decision of the jury. Chambers and Hiss, in other words, had ceased being two men in a court of law, one of whom was lying. Hiss had become a symbol. To those who hated or feared what Hiss symbolized, Chambers was an avenging angel: an odd-looking one no doubt, but still an angel, because avenging. And to those for whom Hiss symbolized something they liked in their country's recent history, he became a martyr, and Chambers the very spirit of evil. Who cared about the verdict of a mere jury, when angels and devils and martyrs were in court?

Those returning soldiers who were angered to find that their country no longer felt "safe" and the soldiers' parents who had been shaken to learn that America could prefer a Harry Truman to a Governor Dewey—both groups found in Hiss a personification of what worried them. He was the New Deal incarnate and also the postwar world, with its nagging, insoluble troubles. He was all the upstart intellectuals, with their complaints and their nostrums, who must somehow be to blame for the withering-away of traditional America. Roosevelt was dead, so it could no longer be his fault that the "right people" were steadily demoted in the hierarchy of power. Harry Hopkins was dead, so it could no longer be his riotous spending of public funds that bought the voters and thus the electors right under the noses of the elite. But the world was still askew, with more and more danger abroad, less respect at home for the old ruling class.

And then came Hiss as a target for their spleen: Hiss, the new ruling class, the man of high-flown theories who had "never met a pay-roll," with a Harvard degree, good clothes, an eastern-seaboard accent, elegant and superior manners—and a traitor! This was the symbol for which they had been groping. It was too good to be true, or rather it was so good that it had to be true.

Overnight, in the imaginations of many pleasant but frustrated men and women, Alger Hiss became an army of people; he became everybody that the American tory had impotently hated. He was the bright young men whose advice had been taken in Washington instead of the advice of the solid business community. He was the writers who had satirized the self-esteem and laughed at the brains of the plutocracy. He was the professors who had taught that America is involved with all mankind and that, in case communism is an enemy, we might as well know something about it. He finally became a large part of the Democratic party, which the old-fashioned middle-western Republicans had always half-felt to be a tawdry mixture of immigrants (who were probably venal) and highbrows (who were probably subversive). And the more Hiss became the personification of the entire post-Hoover revolution, the more appealing became the personification of the good old days: Robert Taft, "Mr. Republican" himself. Taft, of course, was at least as much a product of an eastern-seaboard education as was Alger Hiss, but he dressed with a reassuring sloppiness and spoke with a reassuring middle-westernness, and he didn't believe in foreigners or in anything newfangled. So Evil became more monstrous by the recollection of the Good.

The other group of people, for whom Hiss was a happy symbol, could not understand this concentrated hatred. They saw in him the new type of able young man who was at last taking government service seriously. A generation earlier, he would have stayed at the bar and made a fortune in a downtown New York office. Or in middle life he might have been sent to the Senate (in the days before the popular election of senators) to guard some vast business interest. But in fact he went to Washington, not as the ambassador of a semi-autonomous financial empire, but as a citizen who wanted to work for his government. Many Americans were proud of this change in the social and political climate and liked Hiss as a sign of better times. They could imagine no reason for his becoming a traitor—so lucky a man, so able, and so well thought of—so they refused to believe it. Many of them still refuse, for the evidence, though finally satisfactory to a jury, was far too intricate to satisfy a newspaper-reader who had

no face-to-face knowledge of the witnesses and who did not
choose to be convinced.

Both sides—the haters and the people who thought Hiss a
nice young man—had one point in common: they all saw him
as in some way a shadow of Dean Acheson, a little Acheson
who was easier to shoot at than the big one, if you were a
hater, and all the more necessary to defend if you were on his
side. General Marshall had resigned because of ill-health a
few weeks after Hiss was indicted, and Mr. Acheson had become Secretary of State. Many months were to pass and
much madness was to boil and bubble on the surface of American life before the Secretary himself could be attacked, even
by indirection, as one of the powers of darkness. But Hiss was
the ideal wax image into which the needles of malevolence
might be plunged. He was younger and less important than
Mr. Acheson and probably less able, but they both came
from the same world and shared the same manners—including
the unfortunate manner of talking superciliously to those with
whom they disagreed. They were friends, furthermore, and
Hiss's brother had been a member of Acheson's law firm.
And one of the reasons they were much condemned (or much
admired, as the case might be) was that they looked like
proper, traditional Republicans—America first and no nonsense about the Welfare State—while they preached co-operation abroad and reform at home.

And what about Chambers, the man who destroyed Hiss?

He did not lend himself so easily to symbolism. You might think he was sent from heaven to save America or from hell to denigrate good men, but you could scarcely help wishing that he would go back again to one place or the other, and you would be unlikely to see him as standing for anything typical of your own country. His youth was a squalid misfortune that William Faulkner might have dreamed. As an adult he transcended Faulkner and became a minor figure out of Dostoevski, with several would-be souls warring within his shapeless body. He had the eloquence (at least on paper) and the sudden excitements and the sense of a mission to save men in spite of themselves that we find in so many characters from Russian fiction. He was also sufficiently business-like to be a useful editor on *Time* magazine and sufficiently conscience-stricken to abandon that security in the search for some lonely atonement. Occasionally, when he was not enacting a complicated fantasy to soothe his sense of guilt, he probably meant exactly what he said.

And one day, when he was testifying before the Un-American Activities Committee, when the President had already pooh-poohed the whole matter and Hiss seemed invulnerable, Congressman Richard Nixon became convinced that, against all hope and all probability, this ungainly, heavy-eyed Chambers was telling the truth and that Alger Hiss was simply brazening it out. That was the turning point in three men's careers. Mr. Nixon became a senator and then the Vice-

Hiss, Chiang, Fuchs, and the Bomb

President of the United States; Chambers became a best-selling author; Hiss went to jail. But the wider repercussions of the "Hiss case" were not obvious until the unfortunate man had served at least a year of his sentence.

3

While Alger Hiss was slowly being convicted of perjury, the great Chinese people were rapidly succumbing to their Communist revolution. On the day Hiss was indicted, Mao Tse-tung's armies were pushing far south from Manchuria. In December, 1949, when Dean Acheson had become Secretary of State, the government of Chiang Kai-shek fled to Formosa. And in the following May, when Hiss's first trial began, the victorious Communist general was in Shanghai. The revolution was over. Chiang was undone. The most numerous people in the world had joined what America regarded as the camp of the enemy.

There had been no careful preparation of the public mind for such a catastrophe. Even after the fall of Shanghai no one quite admitted what had happened. It was a time of rumors and of questions that were not answered except by further rumors. (And all the while, here was a man, accused of treason, who had served the Department of State for many years, who had worked in the office of Far Eastern Affairs, who had even been at Yalta, where so many secret concessions were alleged to have been made to Stalin! Could treason be the answer to these accumulating troubles?)

97

The Price of Power

On August 5 the Department of State finally issued a document announcing that Mao Tse-tung was the master of China and that Chiang Kai-shek was in disgrace. The Preface to this paper was an able but belated defense of recent American policy in the Far East.

The public was bewildered, which is always dangerous in a democracy and which is usually the fault of the men in power. The paper might explain and might even justify the actions of the Truman Administration, but no one could explain why the American people had been encouraged ever since Pearl Harbor to soothe themselves with a series of fantasies about China. Franklin Roosevelt may have been the chief culprit, for he really seems to have thought that Chiang Kai-shek's China was, or would someday become, a Great Power. To the mirth of our allies, he treated her as such all during the war. And even as late as the Potsdam conference, Mr. Truman asked the astonished Russians and British to allow the foreign minister of China to assist in making peace treaties for Europe! By that time, even our best friends had given up trying to understand the great American China-myth. In August, 1944, for example, Sir Winston Churchill had sent a minute to his foreign secretary:

"That China is one of the world's four Great Powers is an absolute farce. I have told the President I would be reasonably polite about this American obsession, but I cannot agree that we should take a positive attitude on the matter. The latest

Hiss, Chiang, Fuchs, and the Bomb

information from inside China points to the rise already of a rival Government to supplant Chiang Kai-shek, and now there is always a Communist civil war impending there."

If the American people had been allowed to know, even at the end of the war, what Sir Winston knew from the beginning—that Chiang's China was engaged in a desultory civil war, complicated by a foreign war that she fought when she had time—there would have been less shock and perhaps no search for culprits in 1949. The American government was repeatedly warned by its own agents in China about the strength of the Communists and about the need to persuade Chiang to make popular reforms if he was to be saved at all. But the American people were left with the illusion that the Chinese Communists, if they had any importance, were really discontented agrarians who were not much more dangerous than the followers of William Jennings Bryan. When Major General Patrick Hurley, who had been Secretary of War under President Hoover, went to China in 1944 as the President's personal representative (he later became the American ambassador), he announced to a group of journalists: "The only difference between Chinese Communists and Oklahoma Republicans is that Oklahoma Republicans aren't armed." Meanwhile, as early as 1943, a foreign-service officer had sent to the Department of State an estimate of Chiang's regime that might have been written by Sir Winston himself: "The Kuomintang, once an expression of genuine nationalist

99

feeling, is now an uncertain equilibrium of decadent, competing factions, with neither dynamic principles nor a popular base."

How could the American public judge sensibly? They were told that the Communists were really Republicans and that Chiang was the leader of a "nation" that was a Great Power. In fact, the Communists were really Communists; and Chiang's government was "an uncertain equilibrium of decadent, competing factions"; and China—not yet a "nation" and not yet a Great Power—was on the verge of an irresistible revolution. Except for the fact that the revolution was to prove irresistible, all this was known to every informed person in Great Britain during the war and presumably to every interested person in the Kremlin. Why, then, the American obsession about China?[1]

First, the American people had long been sentimental about the Chinese. We thought they were friends. We thought we had behaved well toward them in the days of "spheres of influence" and of the Boxer rebellion and of agitation for the Open Door. We even thought that they had

1. The British did not deny the potential greatness of China, once united; they merely denied the potential greatness of Chiang Kai-shek. In 1946, Sir Orme Sargent, permanent undersecretary at the Foreign Office, "entered a caveat against the assumption that either the Soviet Union or the United States was necessarily destined to be the greatest Power. There was China, a China awakening from a long sleep, alert, adaptable and quicker in the uptake than any European nation. A China equipped with scores of Krupp and Skoda factories, atomic plants, and limitless man-power, might very soon call the tune to both the United States and the Soviet Union. What was fifty years in modern history—a fleeting moment!" (Sir Robert Bruce Lockhart, *Your England* [London, 1956], p. 217.)

Hiss, Chiang, Fuchs, and the Bomb

accepted our flattering picture of ourselves as an anticolonial power whose interest in Asia was benevolent. So we were surprised to find that the People's Republic hated us; that, instead of seeing us as medical missionaries, friends of Chinese nationalism, and allies in war, they saw us as "Fascist dragons," "capitalist crocodiles," and other unexpected animals. There had clearly been a failure in communication.

Second, because we thought the Chinese were our friends, we took pleasure in imagining that they were a Great Power, even during the war, when we might have noticed that their power was either not great or not used for our purposes. Here, again, Franklin Roosevelt may have misled us. As we have seen, he had an ancient Dutch fear of the British Empire plus an ancient American superstition about the magic of British diplomacy. He wanted, strangely enough, some "balancing" force after the war to prevent Britain from becoming once again too strong. Why not invent China? Why not conceive the "Big Four"? Britain and Russia could indulge their traditional quarrels over the Middle East and the gateways to India, while China and America—friendly and disinterested—would see to it that no great harm was done. (The Department of State, of course, knew better than this. The truth about the postwar balance of power was noted as early as the first Quebec conference. Yet it is hard not to relate President Roosevelt's obsession about the strength of China with his obsession about the latent evils of the British Empire.)

Third, whenever Franklin Roosevelt did or said anything to promote the myth of "China the Great Power" or "China the Great Friend," he could count on Republican support. The Pacific is the ocean of the isolationists, just as the Atlantic is the ocean of the interventionists. We are all the descendants of people who fled from Europe. A few of our ancestors may have come out of curiosity, but most of them came out of poverty or despair or because the police were on their tracks. Our instinctive wish is to be let alone by Europe, to stop fretting about Europe, to turn our eyes toward the Pacific. "Eastward I go only by force," wrote Thoreau, "but westward I go free. . . . I must walk toward Oregon and not toward Europe." That was harmless enough while we were growing up. The adolescent can turn against his family with impunity, because his family is still protecting him—but not so the grown man. We could walk as far as Oregon, but then we had to face about and accept our heritage. We belong to the West, without which we must perish. We do not belong to Asia.

By accident, the Democrats were in power both times we were forced to return to Europe under arms. So the Pacific became not only the ocean of the isolationists, who would shun Europe, but the ocean of the Republicans, whose job it was to find fault with what the Democrats were doing. All during the recent war they complained of the decision to defeat Germany first. We weren't fighting hard enough against Japan, they said; we were neglecting China and starving the armies of General MacArthur.

Thus the China-myth flattered our vanity, suited the President's wartime fantasies, and diminished the Republican attacks on the Administration. But when the myth evaporated and the surprised public asked what had happened to the friendly Great Power they had heard so much about, the Administration was sadly vulnerable. If "our" China never existed, why did Roosevelt affirm it? If it did exist, who sold it to the Communists?

The official explanation put all the blame on Chiang. Since the end of the war the United States had given Chiang more than $2,000,000,000 in grants and credits, plus $1,000,000,-000 of surplus war material that had been sold to the Chinese for $232,000,000. What more could we do? Would further aid on this scale have prevented, or even postponed, the shattering disaster? The State Department answered with an emphatic "No." There was nothing we could do unless we were prepared to fight Chiang's war ourselves: "the only alternative open to the United States was full scale intervention in behalf of a Government which had lost the confidence of its own troops and its own people."

This was doubtless true. Everyone who had reported on China during the previous two years—including General

Wedemeyer, who was in favor of intervention on an immense scale, and Colonel Robert McCormick, who was not—seemed to agree that it was true. But it was also a very sudden surprise for the American people. Equally sudden was the discovery that the Chinese Communists were the real thing and took the Kremlin's view of America. What had become of those agrarian reformers, those Oklahoma Republicans? Had they been invented by the Department of State in order to lull the American people while Chiang Kai-shek was betrayed? And if Chiang was so corrupt and so widely hated, why had we been encouraged to think of him as the "George Washington of China"? These questions were to bedevil Mr. Truman and Mr. Acheson until they both left office. We shall return to them at the time of the crisis over General MacArthur.

4

The anxiety-ridden summer of 1949 not only saw the first trial of Alger Hiss and the final defeat of the armies of the Kuomintang; it also brought the news that an atomic explosion had occurred in the Soviet Union. So the bomb was no longer a monopoly, no longer an insurance, but an immense new risk. And once again came the nagging doubts and suspicions: "Why so soon?" American men of science had thought the Russians would need another three or four years to attain the bomb. Was there a Hiss at Los Alamos who had helped them to beat the timetable? And what about the dread hydrogen bomb? Would Russia now get ahead of us on that?

The second question was answered by President Truman in January, 1950: "I have directed the Atomic Energy Commission to continue its work on all forms of weapons, including the so-called hydrogen or super-bomb." (Professor Einstein commented: "General annihilation beckons.") And the first question seemed to be answered by Dr. Klaus Fuchs, who at this moment confessed that from 1943 until 1947 he had handed to the Russians all the important secrets he could uncover while doing atomic research for the American and British governments.

This was the cruelest blow. Fuchs and Hiss and China; lies and treason and confusion. Was America to be abolished without lifting a finger?

The stage was set for Senator McCarthy.

V

McCarthy and Korea

1

In 1909 Joseph McCarthy was born into an Irish family in northern Wisconsin, a state noted for its German affiliations. He became a lawyer. His professional conduct was so unusual that he was censured by his fellow lawyers. Then he became a judge. His professional conduct was so unusual that he was censured by his fellow judges. In 1942 he joined the Marines, who were too busy to censure him but who must have been surprised by this Intelligence officer who called himself "Tail-Gunner Joe" and who clearly felt that the war in the Pacific had been designed to advance his career. Whatever the design, the result was just as he expected: in 1946 he was elected to the United States Senate (which in due time would also censure him). At once he began looking for something to make a fuss about, something by which to attract wide publicity. He is a burly man, by no means sensitive, but with a disarming boyish grin when life is kind to him.

His first effort to call attention to himself was not good enough, although it may have pleased some of his German-American constituents. In May, 1949, at a Senate hearing he insisted that the brutal conduct of American troops had been the cause of the massacre by German storm troopers of two hundred and fifty Americans and Belgians at Malmédy. A few observant journalists noted that here was a senator who would say anything to make headlines, but, for the rest, this was a vain effort.

In February, 1950, he did better. Speaking to the Women's Republican Club in Wheeling, West Virginia, he tried the subject of traitors, Communist infiltration, and "the bright young men born with silver spoons in their mouths," who, he said, had been disgracing the Department of State. He was off! He had found a subject of such vulgarity and inaccuracy that his mind could grasp it and a subject of such notoriety that he could slake his thirst for fame. Hiss had finally been convicted a few weeks earlier; Fuchs had just confessed; the money for the Marshall Plan was pouring abroad by the thousands of millions; and with the North Atlantic Treaty (ratified in the Senate by a vote of 82 to 13) the United States had joined for the first time in her history an "entangling alliance," a military alliance, with eleven other countries.[1]

We were more and more committed—more and more over-extended, some people said—yet every week we seemed to become less safe. The real reasons for our peril were so complicated and so lacking in popular appeal that they could not be condensed into slogans, so the time was ripe for the purveyors of false reasons. On the famous night in West Virginia when he first attracted attention (for any purpose except that of being censured), McCarthy squeezed the whole of postwar history into one disagreeable idea: "The reason we find ourselves in a position of impotency is not because our only powerful potential enemy has sent men to invade our shores, but rather because of the traitorous actions of those who have been treated so well by this nation. . . . In my opinion the State Department, which is one of the most important government departments, is thoroughly infested with Communists." Then he waved a piece of paper at the audience: a list, he said, of the Communists in the Department of State. The harmless Republican women in West Virginia, who had never met anyone at all like McCarthy, were

1. This was, of course, far more than a mere military alliance. The North Atlantic Treaty Organization, set up primarily to integrate the defenses of the Atlantic nations, has permission to seek also to integrate their economies and thus, by implication, their politics. This larger charge upon NATO may prove to be the last hope of the West, the last escape from suicidal nationalism. The treaty went into effect on August 24, 1949, involving the United States, Great Britain, Canada, France, Belgium, the Netherlands, Luxembourg, Italy, Denmark, Norway, Iceland, and Portugal. Greece and Turkey joined in February, 1952.

naturally impressed. Yet the Senator was waving a letter from James Byrnes, the former Secretary of State, to a congressman called Adolph Sabath—a letter written in 1946 that made no mention of Communists.[2] All he wanted was a document to hold on high; a bill from the nearest bar would have sufficed.

The Senator cannot remember what he said that night. And the Senator's friends deny what the reporters think they heard, which is as follows: "I have here in my hand a list of 205 a list of names that were known to the Secretary of State as being members of the Communist Party and who nevertheless are still working and shaping the policy in the State Department." The next day, when McCarthy spoke at Denver, these Communists had ceased being Communists (like the Oklahoma Republicans of China); they had become "bad security risks." And the day after that, scores of them had disappeared entirely, and what we had left was "fifty-seven card-carrying Communists." As Mr. John Mason Brown puts it, "The pattern of adjustable statistics was set even at the start of the long and loud campaign which was to follow." But the kindly American public would not have been confused by this malevolent nonsense except for the strain of incessant readjustments that it had endured, without rest, ever since Potsdam.

2. The letter dealt with the problem of "screening" four thousand temporary employees transferred from emergency agencies to the Department of State at the end of the war.

Many people wanted an easy explanation. They were glad to hear that frightening events could be charged to an anti-American plot. They welcomed the self-appointed savior who would purge the Department of State, the entertainment industry, and what he called "the whole group of twisted-thinking New Dealers [who] have led America near to ruin at home and abroad." No evidence was asked by McCarthy's followers for the most monstrous charges, because the evidence for treason was felt to be obvious on all sides—in the mounting frustrations and in the fears for the safety of America. "McCarthy may be a little rough," they said, "and at times a little hasty. But someone has got to take on the job of cleaning out this filth."

One can understand these misdirected patriots. One can even sympathize. Suspicion had become an epidemic. No man and no nation should hope to go through life without occasional diseases. Whooping cough must be, and so must Whooping Senators, and from time to time we are likely to catch one or the other. But there should be a doctor at hand to administer to the complaint, which, if caught early, is seldom serious.

The inexplicable fact about McCarthy is not that for seven years he had a following or that the Democratic Administration seemed always on the defensive when answering his charges or countering his fouls. The complaisance of the Senate is what cannot be explained—and the Senate, incidentally, must take full blame for the subsequent complaisance of Mr. Eisenhower, who was not even supposed to know about politics, who certainly did not know about people like McCarthy, and who had therefore to be guided at first by McCarthy's confreres. Yet, with the exception of Senators Benton, Fulbright, and Flanders, the whole of this privileged body of powerful and experienced men seemed to be hypnotized by McCarthy's atrocious talk—or, even worse, they seemed to be afraid. And why hire senators to be afraid?[3]

It was not always thus. When Huey Long—far more able, far more dangerous, than McCarthy—loosed his malignant tongue on Carter Glass of Virginia, Glass remarked on the floor of the Senate that the Romans had once elected a horse to their legislature, thus showing their superiority to the voters of Louisiana—for the Romans had sent the whole horse. The senators used to walk out en masse when Long spoke, in the hope of teaching him better manners. But nobody seemed to care about McCarthy's manners. His combination of rudeness, noise, threats, and effrontery was accepted by his half-stunned associates until he proved himself an even greater nuisance to President Eisenhower than he had been to President Truman. Then, at last, the Senate acted, and McCarthy returned to his appropriate obscurity.

3. The great Vandenberg, who did not scare easily, was mortally ill. He died in April, 1951.

The Price of Power

All this could be explained, although not condoned, if McCarthy's national following had been impressive. But the only impressive thing about him, at the height of his infamy, was that he seemed to scare senators. The outside world, observing this hateful fact, could not be blamed for wondering whether the whole of great America was cowering before an evil fear-monger.

Senators he could scare. And he could scare poor little people who might lose their jobs because of his conscienceless charges. And, as we shall see, he seemed able to scare Mr. John Foster Dulles. But to the responsible press he was always a scandal compounded with a bad joke. Lest we succumb to the legend that he was once an important man (as distinguished from a world-wide disgrace to his country), let us remind ourselves of what we said about him in the days when his star rode high.

The American Political Science Association in 1952 asked its members who specialized in studies of the legislature to list the five best and the five worst senators. At the bottom of the latter list was McCarthy of Wisconsin.

The previous year a magazine had polled the Washington correspondents from all over America, asking them to rate the members of the Senate. At the bottom of the list—with "no competition," according to the magazine—came McCarthy of Wisconsin.

The *New York Times* commented: "If a major objective of

McCarthy and Korea

Russian foreign policy is to undermine the faith of Democratic peoples in their governments, then the Kremlin must rejoice every time that Joseph R. McCarthy opens his mouth in the Senate of the United States." And this was borne out most interestingly by Mr. Herbert Philbrick, a counterspy for the FBI who had worked within the Communist party for nine years. Asked at a press conference what the Communists thought of McCarthy, he answered, "According to the leaders of the Communist Party, McCarthy has helped them a great deal." And he went on to point out in detail, in the *New York Herald-Tribune*, how McCarthy was a boon to the Kremlin.

In 1951 *Time* magazine concluded: "After nearly two years of tramping the nation, shouting that he was 'rooting out the skunks,' just how many Communists has Joe rooted out? The answer is: none." And the *Commonweal*, a Roman Catholic weekly, wrote: "Senator McCarthy acts as he always acts, careless by calculation, ignorant, arrogant, cowardly, and muscular, untrue even to himself, even by whatever peculiar standards, if any, he has set up for himself."[4]

Why, then, was the Senate made timid by this much despised man? At the very start of his notoriety, when his "fifty-seven card-carrying Communists" and his attacks on Professor Owen Lattimore were winning him his first big

4. An entire pamphlet of similar tributes, nation-wide, was compiled in 1952 by the "Wisconsin Citizens' Committee on McCarthy's Record."

headlines, the Foreign Relations Committee of the Senate appointed a subcommittee to inquire into the loose, loud charges. The formidable Senator Tydings of Maryland was chairman, yet McCarthy escaped with his reputation only mildly tarnished, in spite of the fact that he had not been able to prove a single charge. Not only did he escape from an investigation that should have maimed him irrevocably, but he retaliated against Senator Tydings with an unscrupulous violence that left the Senate stupefied.

In the autumn of 1950 Mr. Tydings stood for re-election in Maryland. His seat was thought "safe"; but McCarthy abetted and aided a campaign of defamation, on the grounds of imputed disloyalty, that set new records in abuse and lost Mr. Tydings his seat. The campaign was made especially repulsive by a tabloid, *From the Record*, which did not hesitate to publish a fraudulent composite photograph.

The Senate responded feebly by asking for a report on the election from its Committee on Rules and Administration. The report admitted that "such campaign methods and tactics are destroying our system of free elections and undermine the very foundations of our Government." And it admitted that "the tabloid, *From the Record*, contains misleading half-truths, misrepresentations, and false innuendos that maliciously and without foundation attack the loyalty and patriotism . . . of former Senator Millard Tydings. . . . The publication of any portrayal . . . of the character of the com-

McCarthy and Korea

posite picture as it appeared in the tabloid . . . was a shocking abuse of the spirit and intent of the first amendment to the Constitution."

The report also stated that "Senator Joseph R. McCarthy of Wisconsin was actively interested in the campaign to the extent of making his staff available for work on research, pictures, composition, printing of the tabloid, *From the Record*. Members of his staff acted as couriers of funds between Washington and the Butler campaign headquarters in Baltimore. Evidence showed that some of the belatedly reported campaign funds were delivered through his office." And the report went so far as to say: "We . . . recommend a study looking to the adoption of rules by the Senate which will make acts of defamation, slander, and libel sufficient grounds for presentment to the Senate for the purposes of declaring a Senate seat vacant." But nothing happened.

The most outrageous moments of "McCarthyism" occurred under the astonished gaze of President Eisenhower, and we shall deal with them later. But it is doubtful whether the Senator was ever more seemingly impressive than on the day when, against all precedent and every senatorial tradition (to say nothing of common honesty), he went into another man's state and helped to lie that man into defeat. In fact it was not the impudence of McCarthy that was impressive; it was the silence of the Senate.[5]

5. In these congressional elections of 1950, the Republicans gained 5 seats in the Senate and 28 in the House of Representatives, but the Democrats retained control of both Houses.

115

The Price of Power

2

While McCarthy was busily defaming Senator Tydings' character, the first troops to fight for the United Nations were approaching the Yalu River. Four months earlier, on the evening of June 24, 1950, word reached the Department of State that a North Korean army had invaded the Republic of South Korea. Mr. Truman was at home in Missouri, and Mr. Acheson was at home in Maryland. Within twenty-four hours the President was back in Washington and had soon made his first decision. "The attack upon Korea," he stated, "makes it plain beyond all doubt that Communism has passed beyond the use of subversion to conquer independent nations and will now use armed invasion and war. . . . In these circumstances, I have ordered the United States air and sea forces to give the Korean government troops cover and support." Four days later, on the advice of General MacArthur, Mr. Truman authorized the use of American ground units in South Korea. The die was cast for war on the mainland of Asia.

Meanwhile, the United Nations had been active. Russia had for five months been boycotting the Security Council because of its refusal to seat a representative from Communist China in the place of the representative from Formosa; so the Council called the invasion "a breach of the peace and an act of aggression" and asked for a cease-fire. Thus the President could say that his decision was in accord with the wishes of the United Nations. However, in order to make responsi-

116

bility quite clear, the United Nations ratified the President's decision (or re-ratified it) a few hours after it was announced. And at this time the Council asked that "members of the United Nations furnish such assistance to the Republic of Korea as may be necessary to restore peace and security in the area."

The first response from public opinion, both at home and abroad, was exultant: the right thing was at last being done at the right time. The author of this book was in Paris when the great decisions were made, and that fair city had not known such hope since before the war. A stand had been taken; the old negative pattern had been broken; the United Nations could act; Americans meant what they said! In view of the bitter misrepresentations that were later to be made, especially at home, it is worth recalling Senator Vandenberg's judgment of the opinion of Congress during these first sanguine days. Two months before he died, by which time the waters of good will had been thoroughly muddied, Vandenberg wrote regretfully: "The President's great mistake was in not bringing his Korea decision to the immediate attention of the Congress (as Wilson did at Vera Cruz). At *that* time, the country and the Congress overwhelmingly agreed with him and would have said so. Much of the intervening controversy would have been avoided."

Whence came the controversy? Why did the sense of righteousness and sacrifice turn so sour in so many minds?

The Price of Power

Since every alleged fact has been distorted or denied at some point during the rancorous arguments over Korea, China, Formosa, General MacArthur, Syngman Rhee, Dean Acheson, and an immensely long cast of characters, is there anything we still know for sure?

At Cairo, in 1943, Chiang Kai-shek, Sir Winston Churchill, and President Roosevelt agreed that Korea should be freed when the war ended; she had been for thirty-five years a colony of Japan. Russia accepted the Cairo decision at the Moscow conference of 1945. So when the Japanese were beaten, American troops occupied the country south of the thirty-eighth parallel of latitude, and Russian troops occupied the north. This division was not intended to have any sig-- nificance, at least by the Americans. Someone had to take over while the Japanese withdrew and until the Koreans could reorganize. A year later, after all the disheartening experience with Russia in Europe, the United States announced she would stay in Korea until the country was united and free. In 1947 the vexed problem of Korean independence was put before the United Nations, but Russia would not allow a United Nations commission to visit North Korea. The North Koreans then decreed a "People's Democratic Republic" with jurisdiction over the whole peninsula— whereupon, under the auspices of the United Nations commission, elections were held in the only part of the country where the commission was permitted to operate, and in Au-

McCarthy and Korea

gust, 1948, the Republic of Korea was proclaimed at Seoul, with Syngman Rhee as president.

In 1950, Secretary of State Acheson announced that Korea would now be expected to defend herself but that she was supported by "the commitments of the entire civilized world" under the charter of the United Nations. The last American, and presumably the last Russian, troops were withdrawn, and Korea became in effect two nations, each of which claimed jurisdiction over the other. The Americans promised economic assistance for the Republic of (South) Korea but maintained only a military advisory group in that harassed region. The east-west problem of Germany was thus established on a north-south basis, on a smaller scale but with even subtler complications. In September, 1949, the United Nations commission had reported that it could see no solution to the counterclaims of the Korean Republic at Seoul and the People's Republic in the north, adding that civil war seemed likely.

Although the scale of this new tangle was smaller than that of the vast German problem, it was by no means insignificant. The Korean peninsula is six hundred miles long and, on an average, about a hundred and five miles wide. The population is more than twenty-three million. The country has had an authentic history since the first century B.C. and a misty legendary history a thousand years older. It was the bridge over which Chinese culture was carried to Japan. Its Golden

The Price of Power

Age began a hundred years before Columbus sailed the Atlantic Ocean. And until its recent subjugation by Japan, it had maintained for two thousand years a Confucian father-and-child relationship with China, which has been described as "a never-onerous allegiance to a revered patron." It had suffered, of course, under the usual Asiatic curse of a lazy, feudal nobility and a lazy, corrupt officialdom. But it does not deserve to be dismissed as a ruined, hideous battlefield cluttered with terrified and impoverished "natives," which is all that the American troops could discern upon their arrival.

When President Truman ordered troops to the support of South Korea, he knew this was no place to fight a major war. Indeed, America was in no position to fight a major war anywhere during that summer of 1950, since the President and his Secretary of War, Mr. Louis Johnson, had to a frightening extent dismantled her military power. Within a few weeks of the start of the Korean War, the Administration asked Congress to appropriate $10,000,000,000 for rearmament—at which point some of the first fine enthusiasm for this gallant gesture began to wear thin.

Everyone recognized, therefore, that if Russia or China were to join the war officially, the United States must withdraw. Indeed, five months before the war began, Dean Acheson had explained to the National Press Club that Korea was not part of America's "defensive perimeter." This was the view of the Chiefs-of-Staff as well as of the Department of

McCarthy and Korea

State—a view which, when broadcast to the world, may well have seemed encouraging to the North Koreans.

Why, then, did the United States take the plunge, and why were the American citizens so proud in the first instance? Obviously, we could guard our major interests and protect our mainland without the Republic of (South) Korea. But could we do these things if the world lost faith in the promises of the United Nations and in the firmness of the United States? Dean Acheson, who had made clear that we did not need Korea for our own safety, had also made clear that the safety of Korea was backed by "the commitments of the entire civilized world." What would happen to NATO, our major hope in the West, if we showed ourselves intimidated at the other end of the earth? In New York City the Russians had been doing their best to make a monkey out of the United Nations, producing what its own secretary-general described as "total stalemate." Granted that we could not undertake to fight a great power in Asia, should we therefore throw one more small power to the dogs rather than risk loss of face by attending to our duty?

In a dark hour during the Korean fighting, the President explained to General MacArthur why we had taken up the thankless task: ". . . To lend resolution to many countries not only in Asia but also in Europe and the Middle East who are now living within the shadow of Communist power and to let them know that they need not now rush to come to terms with communism on whatever terms they can get, meaning complete submission.

"To inspire those who may be called upon to fight against great odds if subjected to a sudden onslaught by the Soviet Union. . . .

"To bring the United Nations through its first great effort in collective security and to produce a free world coalition of incalculable value to the national security interests of the United States."[6]

This painful war, which came to seem so useless to so many misled people, was accepted with open eyes, with no illusions, for a purpose that any famous nation in history would praise. The Roman legions in a bleak Northumbrian winter must have grumbled at their tedious "holding operation" against the ferocious Celts, whom they were not even allowed to pursue and annihilate. They must have longed for the comforts and warmth of home. But they were guarding the Wall, the great Wall that ringed the civilized world, behind which developed most of what we now hold dear. They cursed and blasphemed, like the soldiers of the West in Korea, and doubtless they, too, despised the "natives"; but, like the soldiers of the West, they did what was allotted to them, saving the world for as long as possible.

6. These selections are in the form in which General Marshall later released the message—in paraphrase, to protect the code.

McCarthy and Korea

3

The war began with repeated defeats for the South Koreans and for the first bewildered Americans, who had been
doing garrison duty in Japan and who were asked suddenly
to face a horde of well-armed fanatics. The South Koreans,
on the other hand, were far from well armed, although their
training and equipment had been an American responsibility.
We had done a useful job in economic aid but a poor job in
helping the republic to build a modern army. This may have
been partly the result of optimism, in which case the Administration was to blame. But it was chiefly the result of a well-
justified fear that Syngman Rhee, if we helped him to become
sufficiently strong, would solve the problem of unification by
conquering the North. At one point, in fact, we bluntly informed the South Korean government that if it attacked the
"People's Republic" we should end all aid, economic as well
as military.

If the most devoted and industrious army officers, acting
in a strictly advisory capacity, are told not to advise too well
and not to suggest the need for tanks and airplanes for fear
that the advisees might promote a war, they are unlikely to
produce formidable soldiers. And if they ignore the fact that
the terrain is better adapted to guerrilla than to conventional
warfare, this, too, will diminish efficiency. According to an
article in the *New Yorker*, commenting on the first disasters,
"The South Koreans have been trained to maintain fixed

lines, like American soldiers, and it disconcerts them to have anybody at their rear, with the result that they try, somewhat disastrously, to get to the rear of the people at their rear."

No matter whose the fault—and it can never be the fault of untrained and inexperienced soldiers—this is what happened during many depressing weeks. The South Koreans continued "to get to the rear of the people at their rear." And the American garrison troops continued, bravely but at first ineffectively, to learn a rough form of warfare, with no quarter given or imagined, in a rough land of bogs and mountains.

Seoul, the capital of the Republic and only forty miles from the border, fell five days after the invasion. Then the United States Navy was put in to blockade the Korean coast. The whole of our armed forces were now committed—air, land, and sea. Mr. Truman said this was not a war but a police action under the United Nations. But he also announced that the draft would be used to enlarge the American Army.

On July 8, 1950, General Douglas MacArthur was named commander of the United Nations forces. Short of open and official intervention by Russia or by the Chinese, the United Nations could now ill afford to be driven off the peninsula. Yet, by August 6, they were fighting to hold the Pusan beachhead at the southeastern tip of Korea. Here the long retreat ended. Proper arms and large reinforcements had at last arrived from the United States, and the Air Force was supreme. British, French, Dutch, Australian, Turkish, and Philippine troops had also arrived.

After holding for five weeks at Pusan, MacArthur took the offensive, making an amphibious landing at Inchon, on the west coast near Seoul. A few days later the capital was restored to the South Koreans, and the armies of the north, in danger from front and rear, were pouring back across the thirty-eighth parallel. Should they be pursued, or should the "police action" stop at the point where the writ of the police no longer ran? This raised the perplexed question of whether the United Nations were at war. If so, it might be wise to follow the defeated enemy and destroy him. If not, the police would seem to have completed their assignment. But had they?

General MacArthur's orders, as commander for the United Nations, were to "restore peace and security." Could one say this had been accomplished if the North Korean armies were left to reassemble tranquilly and re-equip and wait for the forces of the United Nations to go home? The armies of the free peoples, after all, have proved repeatedly that when the fighting stops they have a tendency to go home. But MacArthur waited on the thirty-eighth parallel, with what for him was great patience, to learn whether he was in command of an army or a group of policemen. On October 7, when South Korean troops had already crossed the parallel,

The Price of Power

the United Nations agreed that the purpose of the entire operation had been "the establishment of a unified, independent, and democratic Korea" and recommended action "to secure stability . . . throughout Korea." General MacArthur was officially notified. He ordered the armies of the United Nations across the border and thereafter assumed that he was at war, that he was under orders to produce a political decision (the unification of Korea) by military means.

The General Assembly of the United Nations is responsible for this recommendation. The Security Council did not discuss it, but neither did it intervene, so it would seem to share responsibility with the Assembly. In spite of his subsequent rash and ill-advised behavior, General MacArthur at this point acted impeccably. He waited for his orders and did what he was told. But then the trouble began. MacArthur had been unleashed—a far more formidable event than the pathetic "unleashing" of Chiang Kai-shek that followed upon the Republican victory in the next elections.

A week before the General Assembly's decision, Chinese Foreign Minister Chou En-lai warned that his country might intervene. The warning was repeated on October 11, with even more than the customary abuse of the United States. On October 15, President Truman met General MacArthur on Wake Island. No one will know for a long time, if ever, who said what to whom on that famous occasion, since the President and the General contradict each other in their reports. But it seems probable that the General thought the Chinese would not intervene and would not be very dangerous if they did. On this advice (assuming it is a correct guess at what was said), the President approved the conquest of North Korea to within a few miles of the Yalu River.

On October 20, the capital of North Korea fell. MacArthur pressed on toward the Manchurian border against a stiffening resistance. On November 24 he issued his order for an "end-the-war" offensive. "They [the troops] will eat Christmas dinner at home," he had announced the previous day. Chinese troops were already heavily engaged, and before the end of the month MacArthur was complaining that he had "an entirely new war" on his hands.

This was an understatement. For weeks the Chinese had been engaged in large numbers but on a scale that might still be ascribed to "volunteers." But on November 26, two hundred thousand men were loosed upon the forces of the United Nations. These were serious troops, not so well equipped as the Russian-trained North Koreans but even more negligent of their own lives. On the western side of the peninsula, the armies retreated after the fashion of a normal defeat, with heavy casualties but with no prospect of disaster. To the east they were fighting front and rear simultaneously and on both flanks. The worst sufferers were in the American First Marine Division, surrounded in a frozen hell of rocky gorges thousands of feet deep, through which the survivors fought their way for forty miles to the sea.

Seoul fell for the second time. But the Communists were no longer fighting garrison troops and ill-trained South Koreans. The lines held, well short of the old beachhead, and in 1951 the forces of the United Nations moved forward again toward the thirty-eighth parallel. But by this time the war between the Administration and General MacArthur was stealing the headlines from the war against the North Koreans.

4

The General is not a good loser. His friends would say that he has not had much practice, but his own theory seems to have been that the many splendid successes in his glamorous life are what anyone would expect from MacArthur, whereas the few spectacular failures are manifestly the fault of somebody else.

The first of these failures was in the Philippines: the day after Pearl Harbor the Japanese were allowed, with one bomber raid, to catch the American Air Force on the ground and to destroy all hope of defending the islands. This was blamed upon General Brereton, although General MacArthur was the man in command. The second grave error was the failure to prepare for the massive Chinese intervention in Korea. He has been accused of provoking that intervention, but this seems unfair. As commander of the United Nations

forces, however, he should have foreseen the danger and been ready for it. He led his troops into a major defeat, yet he put the blame upon the Administration in Washington that would not allow him to turn defeat into victory by bombing the Chinese across the Yalu River, thus extending the war, if need be, into a world conflict on the mainland of Asia. From this time forward, General MacArthur set himself to undo the policy of his Commander-in-Chief and to substitute his own. And he had many busy friends in America who encouraged him in this folly.

On December 6, while the defeat was still in progress, he gave an interview to the *United States News and World Report:*

Q.: "Are the limitations which prevent unlimited pursuit of Chinese large forces and unlimited attack on their bases regarded by you as a handicap to effective military operations?"

A.: "An enormous handicap, without precedent in military history."

Q.: "What accounts for the fact that an enemy without air power can make effective progress against forces possessing considerable air power?"

A.: "The limitations aforementioned, plus the type of manoeuvre which renders air support of ground operations extremely difficult and the curtailment of the strategic potentiality of the air because of the sanctuary of neutrality immediately behind the battle area."

All this was true, but irrelevant. General Omar Bradley, Chief-of-Staff at Washington, was later to reply that spreading the war to China, as MacArthur wished, would lead "to a larger deadlock at greater expense" and "would involve us in the wrong war at the wrong place at the wrong time and with the wrong enemy." Yet MacArthur's many comments to the press during that sad December filled the world with fear. The General was not the only man who underestimated the stubbornness and decisiveness of Harry Truman. British Prime Minister Clement Attlee seems to have assumed that MacArthur could control the President and that, in order to cover up his defeat, he might start dropping atomic bombs on the Chinese. Mr. Attlee flew to Washington to seek reassurance. He might have saved himself the trouble, except that the trip gave grounds for a useful legend in his own party that he had somehow preserved the world from annihilation. Mr. Truman was not to be pushed by anybody.

In March, 1951, when the troops of the United Nations had again made their weary way to the thirty-eighth parallel and the President felt that the time might have come to make a tolerable settlement with the Chinese, General MacArthur made a statement insulting to China and devastating to the policy of his own government. He said that the enemy was "showing less stamina than our own troops under the rigors of climate, terrain and battle." He spoke of "the clear revelation that this new enemy, Red China, of such exaggerated and vaunted military power, lacks the industrial power to provide adequately many crucial items essential to the conduct of modern war." And he offered magnanimously to "confer in the field with the Commander-in-Chief of the enemy forces" in order to realize "the political objectives of the United Nations in Korea," i.e., the unification of the country under Syngman Rhee!

The reaction of the Chinese was violent and bitter, precluding all hope of an early accommodation. The reaction of our own allies was scarcely more favorable, though it was more politely expressed. The reaction of President Truman was conclusive. Eighteen days later he issued a statement: "I have decided that I must make a change of command in the Far East. I have therefore relieved General MacArthur of his commands and have designated Lieutenant General Matthew B. Ridgway as his successor."

VI

"The Mess in Washington"

1

The Korean War or the rearmament that it provoked led to widespread prosperity at home. There were soon sixty-two million men and women at work, although when Henry Wallace had once predicted "sixty million jobs," he was called a moon-faced dreamer. And the Korean War also proved a boon to the American Negro; it brought the beginning of the end of segregation.

In 1948 two events of good omen had occurred: more than a million southern Negroes were able to use the vote that had been so long denied them, and Mr. Truman announced that it was now "the policy of the President that there shall be equality of treatment and opportunity for all persons in the armed forces." This was an Executive Order which was to be "put into effect as rapidly as possible." Nothing much happened except in the Air Force, which was so young that its bad habits were not yet indurate.

"The Mess in Washington"

When the war (or the "police action") began in Korea, the sadly diminished Army had to expand fast. If the young men pouring into every camp as a result of the revived draft were to be trained separately, according to color, long delays must result. But there, on the desk of every commandant, was the Executive Order. And here was the emergency. Officers began to experiment with desegregation, gingerly at first. They found that it worked beyond all expectations. And later, among the desolate hills of Korea, it worked even better. Negroes who were sent to the front as replacements on the same terms as anyone else felt for the first time in their lives that they were American citizens, unqualified. So did the hard-pressed white soldiers who needed them and accepted them as fellow men. Negroes were no longer classified as "unreliable" in combat. They proved to be just like other people in this respect also.

Slowly the idea that integration was possible began to seep into the smaller, more specialized, and therefore more pride-bound Navy and Marine Corps. They, too, were planning to implement the Executive Order, but they might have interpreted "as rapidly as possible" rather languidly had it not been for the war. And as the news of this minor revolution drifted home, most people were glad and found their consciences eased—though some, inevitably, found their prejudices deepened.

This was the only good news to come from Korea. In March and April, 1951, when the troops were back again on the old thirty-eighth parallel, the war seemed endless and began to seem meaningless. Unfortunately, in the week after General MacArthur's dismissal, Senator Vandenberg died at his home in Michigan. There was now no Republican voice to remind the country of its first fine pride in the Korean mission and of its need for unity. The President's mistake in not going to Congress the day the war began, to secure its ready and overwhelming approval, now recoiled upon him. Uncommitted, aware of the public's discontent, the Republicans were free to make this a Democratic war, an "unnecessary war," as Senator Taft said, a war "begun . . . without the slightest authority from Congress or the people."

When the news came that the hero-general had been recalled, Republican leaders in Congress believed that at last they could destroy Harry Truman. Within a few hours they invited General MacArthur to appear before a joint meeting; they agreed to hold an investigation into the entire foreign and military policy of the Administration; and the leader of the House of Representatives, Joseph Martin of Massachusetts, announced that they were considering "the question of impeachments." This dark threat referred to the President and the Secretary of State.

At first, America was on the side of the Republicans. The people had a simple issue, a clear concise deed, on which to vent their pent-up anger. The letters and telegrams to the White House were twenty to one against Mr. Truman—and seventy thousand strong. General MacArthur was given a

"The Mess in Washington"

hero's welcome at San Francisco and again at Washington. On April 19 he appeared before the Congress, "with neither rancor nor bitterness," he said, "in the fading twilight of life, with but one purpose in mind: to serve my country. . . . I now close my military career and just fade away, an old soldier who tried to do his duty as God gave him the light to see that duty."

His method of fading away was to undertake a speaking tour throughout the country, devoted to attacking the Administration and especially to attacking the concept of "limited warfare" that was the essence of the "police action" in Korea. Unlimited warfare against China would mean that all Asia would hate us—yet most of the people in the world live in Asia. And so much of our strength would be committed to this unrewarding struggle that we would be powerless to help Europe should Russia move. Unlimited warfare against Russia might mean the destruction of every center of civilization and of industry. The human race, if there still was one, would then be back at the stage at which the wheel was first invented. Unlimited warfare against North Korea was impossible, since China or Russia or both would intervene. Furthermore, unlimited warfare against anybody would lose us our Western allies. Yet this impatient old General, exasperated by the failure to end his career in a blaze of triumph on the Yalu River, preached up and down the country that limited warfare was "appeasement of Communism."

That immature, anarchic doctrine was received with cheers.

The Price of Power

The public longed for an answer to the unanswerable. The thought of America trapped in a stalemate, helpless to get her own way, no matter what move she made, seemed intolerable. We had forgotten the meaning of "police action." We had forgotten that the United Nations were guarding the Wall and that guardians cannot go home when they become bored, lonely, cold, and miserable. Neither can they ravage the world, until there is nothing left to guard, out of sheer frustration. "There is no substitute for victory," said the General. He was wrong. He should have said there is no such thing as victory for those who are protecting civilization. The day never comes when they can down arms, with the job well done. Perhaps that is why the Romans grew tired in the end and gave up trying; but at least they held the Wall for four hundred years.

Mr. Truman must share the blame for the misunderstanding that General MacArthur fed and flattered. From the first days in Korea, the President should have explained and re-explained the meaning of "limited warfare." He should have called in the Republican leaders, committing them irrevocably to the great design. He should have been Arthur Vandenberg in addition to Harry Truman—a large assignment but worth trying, in view of the stakes.

√ Mr. Truman played his hand well, politically. The old soldier, if he did not fade away, at least blew over and ceased being a nuisance to anybody. But he left behind him the feeling that, even if he had been wrong this time, "limited warfare" was also wrong. Mr. Truman knew better, and Mr. Acheson. They should have taught the public, day in and day out, that a small defensive war, which drags on discouragingly and which ends in, at best, a graceless truce, may be our only substitute for the big war that ends in annihilation. The world that the mathematicians and the physicists have invented is no place for people who believe in "victory." ↙

The Senate hearings on the "MacArthur scandal," which the Republicans thought would put an end to Harry Truman, left the General at least half-faded. The public learned to its amazement that the Joint Chiefs-of-Staff were unanimous in support of the President. General MacArthur, they all three testified, was mistaken in his policy, which was to blockade the Chinese coast, encourage Chiang Kai-shek to be as bothersome as possible, and bomb the Chinese bases in Manchuria. This meant the unlimited war that they were resolute to avoid. But the General, they added, was worse than mistaken in disobeying orders and disregarding the policies of the Administration. This was an attack on the Constitution of the United States.

No matter how unpopular Mr. Truman might be, the Constitution was not unpopular. The General's reputation was damaged by such testimony. Nevertheless, at the end of the hearings eight Republican members of the committee signed a statement denouncing the Administration, the dismissal of the

General, the policy in the Far East, and the concept of limited warfare "with no positive plan for achieving a decisive victory." And that was the end. Feelings may have been eased by this futile attack. There was no more talk of MacArthur for President or of impeachments. The hero-worship had subsided; yet Mr. Truman did not gain in popularity. Nobody seemed to like anybody very much in the spring of 1951.

In June of that year McCarthy erupted, making a sixty-thousand-word speech in the Senate in which he said that General Marshall was part of "a conspiracy so immense, an infamy so black, as to dwarf any in the history of man." The idea seemed to be that the General was planning to sell his country to the Communists at home and to the Russians abroad. Perhaps the senators thought that McCarthy had gone mad and could now be trusted to abolish himself. In any case they allowed him to make these charges unreproved—a decision that they were to regret.

2

Korea, communism, and corruption: these were the Republican war cries for the campaign of 1952. They were a powerful combination, especially when summed up under the simple heading "the mess in Washington."

The Democrats had unluckily been exposed by some of their associates to the perfectly fair charge of corruption. The corruption was not very great, but it was well publicized, and it was undeniable. The truth of this charge lent a spurious air of authenticity to the charges about Korea and communism, which might otherwise have been explained away, since the first was based on a misunderstanding of the nature of the war and the second was based largely on the unhappy phrase "red herring." But the corruption was a fact.

Early in 1950 a subcommittee of the Senate unearthed the famous "five per centers," who for this modest cut were prepared to use their friendship with government officials, especially in the procurement sections of the armed forces, to facilitate contracts. Having been exposed, those people might have been suppressed and forgotten after a few days of headlines had it not been for Brigadier General Harry Vaughan —the President's old friend and military aide—who had been given a "deep-freeze" by a company that might well have been thankful for a kind word in the right quarter.

Harry Vaughan was rough and noisy and amusing. Mr. Truman had known him well and liked him much ever since army days during World War I. And Mr. Truman, as his biographer admits, "could sometimes stand some pretty commonplace company." The press secretary to the White House, according to this biographer, "developed a saying when adverse publicity appeared, 'Cherchez le Vaughan.' " This "deep-freeze" became a symbol for a slackness that was unjustly attributed to all the President's "old cronies."

Then came the mink coat: the wife of a former examiner of loans for the Reconstruction Finance Corporation had been "helped" to buy a mink coat by the attorney for a firm that was asking the RFC for a loan. Senator Fulbright's investigations had already shown that the chairman of the Democratic National Committee had "helped" to secure a similar loan for a company that had retained him as its attorney. So the mink coat joined the deep-freeze as a sign of "the mess in Washington."

And the "mess"—which, so far as corruption went, was deplorable, but on a modest scale—was soon vaguely extended to include all the rasping troubles of the day: the weary negotiations with the North Koreans at Panmunjom, month after month, that never led to a cease-fire but that procured from the enemy a "final" list of three thousand American prisoners out of the eleven thousand recorded as missing in action. (Had the rest been murdered?) And all the time, in the background, was the steady rattle of accusations about "softness toward communism"—the horrid suspicion that the country might, after all, be the victim of a great plot. How could the Senate, people asked, have accepted McCarthy's speech about General Marshall unless there was "something in it"? Not the great General of the Army, doubtless, but what about the people around him?

America was still in an ugly mood when the time came for the nominating conventions of 1952. Yet, in spite of Mc-

"The Mess in Washington"

Carthy's coming indignities—which were doubly shocking because of their effect abroad—this was to prove the low point. The country chose two good candidates and began to work itself off the mudbank.

Most Americans and all foreigners make fun of the national conventions, which are certainly indecorous but not necessarily the worse for that. The American political party is a congeries of state, county, and city machines, which have conflicting interests and divided counsels. Normally, it has no unity of ideas or principles, as is shown in both parties today by the regional responses to the Negro problem. A convention is a parley of local bosses and their hangers-on, each group representing the desires and the prejudices of its own region. Since the regions may be as far apart in miles and in climate as Dublin is from Magnitogorsk in the Urals, the hopes and the hatreds may also be far apart.

The first job of the convention is to find a candidate who is not too much disliked by any of the state, county, or city groups. This is not easy, except on the rare occasions when an Eisenhower is at hand. And, second, the convention must create the fiction of unity in a party that is a sprawling collection of disparate groups. The fiction must last until November, and it must persuade the rank and file of party workers that they have common loyalties and ambitions in addition to their common distaste for the enemy. Hence the singing and the revelry and all the clownishness that some people deprecate. Woodrow Wilson, who was one of the deprecators, lamented that the "President is chosen, not by proof of leadership among the men whose confidence he must have . . . but by management—the management of obscure men—and through the uncertain chances of an ephemeral convention which has no other part in politics." Nevertheless, odd as the system can be made to sound, it often works. And it worked in 1952. ✓

The Republicans met at Chicago in early June. There they played for the last time their customary drama of almost nominating Robert Taft. It was a sad little play, because everyone knew it had an unhappy ending and most people wished it didn't. They would truly have liked to nominate Taft. They acknowledged his leadership, and they respected it—not only the five hundred "ultras" who voted for him on the first and only ballot, but more, far more, than were needed to give him the six hundred and four votes that would have meant victory. But they felt, regretfully, that he could not win. So they nominated General Eisenhower, whom they did not know, around whom were gathered no ancient loyalties, but who was vastly popular and under whose leadership they could claim a "new" Republicanism. Not that most of them wanted any such thing; but they did want office, and the "old" Republicanism, which in their hearts they loved, seemed an inadequate vote-getter.

When the Governor of Illinois, Mr. Adlai Stevenson, wel-

"*The Mess in Washington*"

comed the Democratic delegates to the same hall in Chicago later in the same month, he commented on the Republican convention. "For almost a week," he said, "pompous phrases marched over this landscape in search of an idea, and the only idea they found was that the two great decades of progress in peace, victory in war, and bold leadership in this anxious hour were the misbegotten spawn of socialism, bungling, corruption, mismanagement, waste and worse. . . . After listening to this procession of epithets about our misdeeds, I was even surprised the next morning when the mail was delivered on time!"

This was pleasing and wholly unlike the conventional speech of greeting, "which brings sweet sleep down from the blissful skies." Even more remarkable, however, was the speaker's demand that the delegates think hard and with fresh imaginations: "We want no shackles on the mind or spirit, no rigid patterns of thought, no iron conformity. We want only the faith and conviction that triumph in free and fair contest. . . . Self-criticism is the secret weapon of democracy."

Since Mr. Stevenson hoped to avoid the nomination and to continue his work as governor of Illinois, he must sometimes have regretted that speech. The delegates found themselves lifted into a sharp, clean, unaccustomed air, where their spirits could expand magnanimously. They liked the feeling, and Mr. Stevenson lost his chance to carry on with the governorship. He was nominated on the third ballot. In his speech of acceptance he asked the delegates and the listening nation to face some cold truths: "The ordeal of the twentieth century—the bloodiest, most turbulent era of the Christian age—is far from over. Sacrifice, patience, understanding and implacable purpose may be our lot for years to come. Let's face it. Let's talk sense to the American people."

No one could call the nation morally decrepit when its candidates for the highest office were General Eisenhower and Governor Stevenson—both modest men, both representing the abiding virtues of their country, both sickened by the blathering of vulgar senators, and both of a commanding authority. The General's authority sat easily upon him, except when he was making a speech written by someone else; then the audience was inclined to fidget but never to forget that it was watching a man who had made history. The Governor's authority blazed forth when he began a speech; the listeners awoke, delighted, to the knowledge that this unpretentious and almost diffident man—whom most of them had never seen, even in the picture magazines—could bring them to a new pride in the long task that faced America, giving dignity and meaning to their frustrations.

The Democratic campaign was confused by Mr. Truman, who seemed to think he was still running for office and that General Eisenhower could be treated like the much-abused Eightieth Congress. If a voter grew weary of being asked by

"The Mess in Washington"

Governor Stevenson to take the high line, he could attend President Truman's meetings, where the Republicans were attacked with a disrespect that recalled their own language about Dean Acheson. This made for untidiness.

The Republican campaign, meanwhile, was confused by Senator Taft, who sought to impose isolationism upon a candidate who was a symbol of world responsibility, and by Senator McCarthy, who had called George Marshall a traitor and who sought to impose a rowdiness that offended every instinct of General Eisenhower. This, too, made for untidiness—especially when the General was induced to lend a hand in McCarthy's difficult campaign for re-election and thus to refrain from defending George Marshall in the state of Wisconsin. Few Republican politicians would have advised differently. The Senate, according to all predictions, would be closely divided, even if the Republicans won. If McCarthy lost his seat, as he looked like doing unless the presidential candidate came to his rescue, the Senate (and thus the chairmanships of the all-powerful committees) would be handed to the Democrats.

In making this heavy decision to support this disreputable senator, the General relied on his new friends in a world where he found himself a stranger. No one could have foreseen the enormities that McCarthy would commit on his return to the Senate. Indeed, if Taft had not died in the early months of the new Administration, McCarthy might have been held somewhat under control. Senator Taft was an honorable man. Having made his peace with the President, he would do his best to add luster to the first Republican government in twenty years. And there could be no luster, not even a modest dignity, while McCarthy went unsuppressed.

In spite of many hard words off-stage, this was not an unpleasant campaign. The two candidates, at least, worked faithfully to remind the people of the dignity of the predicament in which they lived. The nation was more united and more thoughtful on the morning after election day than it had been for many discordant years. The General received 33,927,549 votes, and Governor Stevenson received 27,311,-316: 442 votes in the electoral college for the Republicans, 89 for the Democrats. Thirty-nine states had voted for the General, nine for the Governor—a nation-wide victory that recalled the early days of Franklin Roosevelt. Yet the Republicans held the Senate precariously: 48 to 47, with 1 independent. In the House of Representatives, 221 Republicans faced 212 Democrats.

V I I

The Making of a President

1

As early as 1947, General Eisenhower described himself to a friend as "just a good Kansas Republican." This might explain his lack of interest when offered the nomination by President Truman. But, aside from casting occasional Republican votes, he did not allow himself to take a clear political stand until he left the army temporarily to become president of Columbia University. Then it became obvious, from many casual remarks, that he was something far more old-fashioned and far more interesting than "a good Kansas Republican": he was a Whig.

For thirty years before the Civil War, the Whigs had been the opposition party to the Democrats. In New England, as in the Deep South, they were the party of the well-to-do and the respectable. (When the beautiful Miss Howell of Mississippi met Jefferson Davis, whom she was soon to marry, she wrote that he was the first Democrat she had ever seen who was a gentleman.) Heirs to the Federalists and forefathers of the Republicans, the Whigs had one distinctive doctrine that was all their own, that would have been repudiated with equal vigor by Alexander Hamilton, who built the ancestral party, and by Abraham Lincoln and Theodore Roosevelt, who adorned the party of the descendants: the Whigs believed that the powers of the presidency should be kept as small as possible. The famous Whigs are senators such as Henry Clay and Daniel Webster. Most people would have trouble in remembering the Whig Presidents. The very name is a sign of distrust in the Executive: the first American Whigs rebelled against the distant stubborn power of King George, so the enemies of "King Andrew Jackson" called themselves Whigs, claiming that he was making the President an elective monarch.

In 1840 the Whigs elected William Henry Harrison, an aging warrior who had been told by his campaign managers "not to say a single word about what you think now or will do hereafter." He was chosen by the people on the ground that his favorite drink was hard cider, whereas his opponent preferred champagne, which suggested foreigners and was wicked. So he had no great promises to redeem, between drinks, and was expected to sit quietly in the White House while the Senate ran the country.

Harrison's inaugural address, which was the work of

The Making of a President

Daniel Webster, might have changed history and revised the uses of the Constitution had the new President not died within a month of taking office. The address said that the presidency was not intended to be a center of power, as Jefferson had shown it to be with his silent manipulations and as Jackson had shown it to be with his direct appeals to the people. According to Harrison, his only task was to execute the laws that Congress handed to him. He promised not to use the vast influence inherent in the federal patronage and in his own position as the one man elected by the entire nation— the one man responsible to everybody. In other words, he said he would never seek to impose his will on Congress.

We have had Presidents who conformed to this Whig pattern, but they have done so by accident, because they were incompetent to do anything else. The strong Presidents, hitherto, have acted according to Theodore Roosevelt's boast: "I did not usurp power, but I did greatly broaden the use of executive power." Each dangerous moment in American history has brought a little more power to Washington, at the expense of the state governments. And in Washington the new power tends to gravitate toward the White House, to the annoyance of senators. Yet, in spite of this steady drift, there has always been a public that resents the new executive powers and that looks backward longingly toward the Whig theories. The purpose of the Constitution, these people believe, is to make government very slow and very difficult, so that the major regions of the country and the major interests may be protected from sudden popular excitements. Executive power is swift, whereas power dispersed through a loosely organized Congress, devoid of party discipline, is reassuringly slow.

In the past the people who took this view have had their way whenever the President was too unimportant to make use of his office. With General Eisenhower, for the first time, a President of great authority and popular appeal has carefully refrained from power. This explains his *rapprochement* with Senator Taft.

After his defeat at the Republican convention and before deciding to take part in the campaign, Taft called on the General for breakfast at Columbia University. He brought with him a manifesto, and when he left, he announced that the candidate was "in full agreement" with it, except for "differences of degree" in foreign policy. Governor Stevenson called this a "great surrender." Many liberal Republicans were shocked, thinking that the General had accepted Taft's ideas in order to win Taft's aid.

But if we look at the manifesto in the light of the last four years, we see that the General made no concessions of principle. Obviously, the two men would never agree on foreign affairs: Taft could not see the need for foreigners, whereas the General had learned that they could be most useful, as well as agreeable. In domestic policy, however, the two men saw eye to eye: Taft had simply written down what the less articulate General would have expressed less clearly.

The theme of the manifesto was "liberty against creeping socialism," which meant drastic reduction in spending and in taxes—i.e., less government. "General Eisenhower agrees," wrote Taft, "that the proper role of the Federal Government beyond its present activities is one of advice, research and assistance to the states, the local communities and the people." Furthermore, "General Eisenhower has told me that he believes strongly in our system of Constitutional limitations on Government power and that he abhors the left-wing theory that the Executive had unlimited powers." Here is the "co-operation" with senatorial ambitions that Clay and Webster had hoped to exact from the pliant Harrison but that had never before been offered gratis by a President of stature. The offer was made out of deep conviction. The General intended, as far as possible, to reverse the trend toward the presidential form of government and to revert to a constitutional theory that would have delighted Henry Clay. But how far was it possible?

A proof of the sincerity of the President's Whig theories was given when Senator Taft died, in July, 1953. The Senate had to choose a new Republican leader—and the party leader in the Senate has sometimes the power to make or break an Administration. Yet President Eisenhower told his Cabinet that the Administration must remain strictly neutral. He urged them to avoid even the most indirect expression of a hope as to whom the Senate might choose. The prerogatives of the Congress were inviolate and were no concern of the Executive.

The men who devised the Constitution may well have believed that this was how the division of powers would work. But they were wise men. They knew that the twentieth century might be unlike the eighteenth, and they wrote a document that could be interpreted and reinterpreted as the future saw fit. The future, on the whole, has been on the side of Presidents who did not refuse power. Mr. Eisenhower's self-denial, for better or for worse, led to the choice of Senator Knowland of California, a strong and able man, but the leader of the Chiang gang, who has been described as "the Senator from Formosa." And the same self-denial encouraged McCarthy.

✓ Never has a grave decision, made in the name of political expediency, been punished more quickly than the decision to support McCarthy for election in Wisconsin. The new Administration was scarcely under way when the Senator began his attack on the information services of the United States. In no time he had made his country a joke throughout Europe, demonstrating meanwhile that Secretary of State John Foster Dulles lacked authority and that the Whig theory of the presidency is no good for the twentieth century. (It was no good for any century, as our history proves.) Power is there

the damned power

to be used. If no one else will use it, the worst man present is always glad to oblige.

There had been no charges of communism in the overseas libraries and news services or in the "Voice of America" broadcasts. There was no remote chance that McCarthy's conduct could be serving a useful purpose. He was simply proving his power by challenging the right of the President and the Secretary of State to make foreign policy. The President did nothing, because he did not believe the Executive should "interfere" with the Senate—even when a senator interfered with the Executive to the extent of making it ridiculous to all the world. And the Secretary of State did nothing, presumably because he was scared. He had only to say "Stop it!" and the Senator would have stopped. McCarthy could have gone on investigating things and calling names as long as the Senate itself permitted. This was a pity but not a catastrophe. What disgraced America was the fact that he gave orders to the Department of State: "Hire this man, suspend that man, remove these books from our libraries, cancel those directives!" (McCarthy did not order books to be burned. That was an extra touch provided by the Foreign Service, in the hope that the Senator would be pleased.)

Under the Constitution, McCarthy's right to give these orders was the same as that of any coal miner in West Virginia. Yet he gave them, and John Foster Dulles cowered and did what he was told. The cowering went so far that the de-

department suspended the head of its International Broad-
casting services because he had questioned, in a private memo-
randum, McCarthy's suggestion that the "Voice of America"
should refrain from quoting "controversial" authors. The
"suggestion" was adopted with obsequious speed, and the
man who called attention to its folly was suspended—just in
case McCarthy might some day hear that somebody in the
Department of State dared to disagree. This was an open re-
nunciation of human dignity. If responsible public officials
insisted on lying down in the mud in front of McCarthy,
why should he refrain from stepping on them?

This wretched scene was witnessed by Raymond Aron of
Figaro, a Frenchman who had been a friend and defender of
the United States. Americans abroad have often been thankful
to him for his understanding and his interpretations of our
country. But this time he, too, had "had enough." In an interview before leaving Washington for Paris, he said he could
no longer defend the United States from the charges of fear,
of hysteria, and of the inner weakness and unreliability from
which fear and hysteria spring. Yet the true state of affairs
was less unhealthy than M. Aron thought. America was not
hysterical. The horrid little drama that disillusioned him
could be explained by the juxtaposition of an abnormal senator who might not have been there without the President's
help, a President so new to the White House that he chose
not to use his powers, and a Secretary of State who was either
frightened or negligent.

The Making of a President

McCarthy, true to form, lost no time in taking advantage of the Administration's weakness. Having walked tentatively upon Mr. Dulles' prostrate body, he began jumping up and down. He sent his Buffoon Boys to Europe: Cohn and Schine. As Richard Rovere commented at the time: "In the basic circumstances of the trip there was the ready-made plot for a gorgeous farce: two young men madly, preposterously bent on the ideological purification of the greatest government on earth. Writers of fiction value such ideas so highly that they sometimes haul each other into court over them."

The entire journey of these maladjusted children was unabashed slapstick. And the nations of Europe, who had received with half-grudging thankfulness the vast benefactions from America, were in a mood to laugh uproariously. The joke was not very useful to the great republic that permitted it. Yet it was typical of McCarthy, who has an infallible instinct for debasing everything dignified and venerable in his country: the Constitution, the President, the universities, General Marshall, and a long list of men who stand for duty and honor and intelligence. He personifies the grumbling revolution, never far from the surface, against decorum and propriety.

McCarthy's next attack on the Executive, in February, 1954, was directed against the Army—or rather against a dentist in the Army who was accused of Communist affiliations. He had refused to answer certain questions before a Senate subcommittee on the grounds that the answers might incriminate him. In other words, he had appealed to the Bill of Rights, which is imbedded in the Constitution and which was long the proudest boast of our people, but which Mc-Carthy regards as a discreditable aberration on the part of our ancestors (the attack, as usual, was upon tradition, law, and due process—the basis of freedom). McCarthy seemed equally furious with the Army for having let this dentist in and for having allowed him to depart with dignity. In the course of the hearings, he attacked a brigadier general in these words: "You are a disgrace to the uniform. You're shielding the Communist conspirators . . . you're not fit to be an officer. You're ignorant."

Although once again nothing happened, although the Secretary of the Army proved as pliant as the Secretary of State, these words were the turning point in McCarthy's career. The brigadier had been obeying an Executive Order when he refused certain information and provoked this outburst. The President was not pleased. If an Army officer could not follow the orders of his Commander-in-Chief without being black-guarded by this upstart from Wisconsin, perhaps the time had come to assert the might of the Executive. From that day forward the Administration moved against McCarthy—very gently, it seemed, but the gentlest move sufficed, as any of the President's great predecessors could have told him.

In March, 1954, the Army charged that Senator Mc-Carthy, the staff director of his subcommittee, and little Roy

The Making of a President

Cohn of the variety team had sought to obtain preferential treatment in the Army for Private David Schine, who had recently been drafted. McCarthy replied, inevitably, that the Army was trying to blackmail him into dropping an investigation into communism at Fort Monmouth. The Senator's own subcommittee decided to investigate. The hearings, which were televised, dragged on for more than a month. Nobody proved anything, in a legal sense, but the big public had a chance to watch McCarthy in action.

This was not a pretty sight. At one point he sought to discredit the Army's attorney, Mr. Joseph Welch, by attacking a young member of the attorney's firm on the ground that he had once belonged to the National Lawyers Guild, which had Communist connections. For the first time, when the reputation of this innocent and wholly uninvolved young man was heedlessly attacked before a national television audience, Mr. Welch seemed to understand what manner of man he was examining. The care for human dignity and for justice (on which civilization rests and which McCarthy derides) was then demonstrated before the nation-wide public. Astonished, as if he had suddenly faced the ghost of some long-buried evil, Mr. Welch spoke softly: "Little did I dream you could be so reckless and so cruel as to do an injury to that lad. . . . If it were in my power to forgive you for your reckless cruelty, I would do so. I like to think I am a gentle man, but your forgiveness will have to come from someone other than me. . . . Have you no sense of decency, sir, at long last? Have you left no sense of decency?"

The television cameras are as cruel as fate. There is no escaping what they put before your eyes. Here was the homely goodness that men revere faced with the barbarism of which men are ashamed. The innocence of Mr. Welch, who saw McCarthy clear for the first time, was the deadliest part of the picture. The Army had gained its revenge.

The end of the squalid tale came a few months later. The Senate was at last emboldened to act. In September, 1954, it appointed a select committee to report on Resolution 301: "That the conduct of the Senator from Wisconsin, Mr. McCarthy, is unbecoming a member of the United States Senate, is contrary to senatorial traditions, and tends to bring the Senate into disrepute." Here were no stunts, no cameras, no comic "points of order," no Cohns, no Schines, no levity. The Senate was reassuming its dignity and reasserting the traditions of a country that McCarthy had never found time to understand during his brief, pushful career. The adverse vote was 67 to 21. This was the fourth senator to be censured in 167 years.

McCarthy, who had already insulted the President by changing his "twenty years of treason" (meaning the Democrats) to "twenty-one years of treason," now "apologized" to the country for having supported General Eisenhower in 1952. The country was not interested. Within a few months a Washington correspondent wrote that "a ghost walked in" when McCarthy appeared at a hearing of a senatorial subcommittee.

2

We have gone ahead of our story by following McCarthy into his ghostly decline. But the McCarthy challenge illustrates a main problem of the Administration: How self-denying, in terms of power, could the President afford to be? How long could he cling to his Whig theories?

In the spring of 1951, when the country was outraged by the news that Mr. Truman had discharged General MacArthur, a cartoon appeared with the pleasing caption: "Who does Harry Truman think he is—the President?" The answer was "Yes; very much so"—which was the reason for his success. In the spring of 1954, Mr. Eisenhower was struck with the same dynamic idea. And it was high time, for in the absence of executive authority a new "mess in Washington" was developing: Republicans attacking Republicans, congressmen attacking the Cabinet, everyone angry, and nothing done on the Administration's program. A Republican magazine, *Business Week*, raised the question "whether the Republicans are equal to the responsibility of power." And the *New York Herald-Tribune* wrote: "The effect of this new kind of 'mess' is to exhibit the Republican Government as quarrelsome, unproductive and legislatively nearly impotent."

The Price of Power

In fact, it was a very old kind of mess, the oldest in American history. Whenever a weak President sits in the White House, the Congress degenerates into "a scuffle of local interests," and the public business does not go forward. The "new" factor in the situation was that the President was weak on purpose—not because he was made that way but because he thought it was his duty. Luckily, he learned that it was not. But, first, in addition to the woe that was McCarthy, he had many disillusioning experiences.

He was deeply hurt, for example, in the summer of 1953, when Congress paid no heed to his advice and recommendations on the Mutual Security Program and on other matters touching the safety of the nation. Here, surely, he was an expert. He thought if he made known his judgment to the Congress, which was controlled by his own party, it would at once take action. But Congress does not operate like that. Until the President is ready to insist and to use the prestige of the only man who represents the entire nation, Congress gives itself to parochial affairs and to avoiding anything that might alienate the home-town vote.

The President was also unhappy at finding that many of his opinions were more acceptable to the Democrats than to the Republicans. He had pictured himself as the leader of a loyal group. He was ready to be most modest in his leadership, to consult always with the elders of the party, to accept advice, and to give credit to other people. But his alleged followers ignored him or opposed him openly, while his alleged opponents were on his side. During 1953, Democratic votes in Congress saved the Administration from defeat on fifty-eight occasions. This was very confusing—so confusing, in fact, that Mr. Eisenhower was driven to consider a most rash plan: the founding of a third party.

The President knew that he represented a popular desire both deep and important—for a relaxation of tension, for a renewal of trust in the traditions and purposes of the national community, for an escape from the mean-spirited years of suspicion when sensible men half-believed that the country was infected with plots and treasons. He knew that the people trusted him. He felt that if he were allowed to go forward with his unambitious program, he could revive that sense of unity for which most men longed.

The Republican Congress thwarted him, disregarding his requests, prolonging the indecorous days of accusations, investigations, and red herrings galore. So he began thinking about a new party, in which men of sober and conservative temperament might come together to bring tranquillity to America. Fortunately, his good sense persuaded him that he must stick to the hard task of using the machinery at hand, of reanimating the Republican party with a philosophy fit for the twentieth century. This was indeed a hard task; yet it was not impossible, once he set his mind to it, whereas a third party would have repeated the sad mistake of Theodore

Roosevelt in 1912. The Eisenhower Republicans would have been destroyed by the party machine; the "unreconstructed" Republicans, the heirs of Robert Taft, would have been left in control.

The first Roosevelt—the master craftsman at finding a middle ground that could unite the largest possible number of hitherto discordant groups—formed his new party in 1912 at the height of his popularity and received more votes than the Republicans. All he accomplished was to hand the election to Woodrow Wilson and to hand the control of every state, county, and city machine to the very Republicans he was seeking to overthrow. And they were never ousted from power, from that day until the rise of General Eisenhower. Had the General, discouraged and dismayed, followed in Theodore Roosevelt's footsteps, he would have lost his chance of ever ousting or converting these outmoded men. The nation would have remained cruelly divided.

Because of the President's wise decision, the American political system has returned, for the time being, to its normal shape. The two parties stand for slight variations on the same program. Voters may feel passionately that one party will do the job well, the other badly; but there is no large division as to the nature of the job. People may deplore this or that member of the government or of Congress, but hardly anybody deplores the broad purposes of the Administration. Those who call the government weak and fumbling mean that they want it to do the accepted task faster and better.

The Making of a President

Because of the President's decision to remain the leader of a deeply rooted national party, he has become a symbol of unity instead of becoming the cause of hates and discords. He is clearly more popular than the party he leads. He can use this popularity to whatever extent his conscience and his modesty permit.

And because of the President's decision, he was bound to attempt a second term if possible. No one could pretend that he has imposed a new pattern on the Republican party to date. But, once he undertook the job, no one could expect him to leave it half-done—fate permitting.

VIII

"Peace" and the Bandung Conference

1

Aside from the accidents to his health, Mr. Eisenhower has been a lucky President. A tendency to good luck is important for politicians. The most striking proofs of this statement during the first two years of the new regime were the death of Stalin in 1953 and the defeat of the Republicans in the mid-term elections of 1954. The first made possible a bloodless end to the fighting in Korea. The second made possible a genuine *détente* at home. And this, in turn, made possible the rise of General Eisenhower as a man above parties and very nearly above criticism—a father-figure for the nation.

During the campaign of 1952 the Republicans promised to end the war in Korea, balance the budget, halt inflation, and reduce taxes. They also charged that the Democrats had waged war in Korea "without the will to victory . . . and by their hampering orders [had] produced stalemates and ignominious bartering with our enemies." This seemed to mean that the war must be "ended" by adopting General MacArthur's pleas and abolishing all "hampering orders." Was Korea to be unified for Syngman Rhee, heedless of war in Asia? This is what Senator Knowland half-demanded, and Senator Jenner of Indiana and Senator Malone of Nevada. Even Senator Taft said that a settlement that left Korea divided would be "extremely unsatisfactory." There was much talk about "stopping the spread of Asiatic Communism." Aside from killing all Asiatics, no one suggested how this was to be done.

The President disagreed with these Republican senators. He admitted that a further stalemate would alienate Congress and might destroy the Administration, but a final thrust for military victory would be expensive and dangerous. He thought that even an advance of ninety miles, to the narrow waist of the peninsula (leaving a buffer between the armies and the Yalu River), would cost about $4,000,000,000. And such an advance, he knew, might bring war with China. So he espoused the "limited victory" that Republicans had scorned during the campaign.

The first step toward "limited victory" explains what Mr. Dulles must have meant when he spoke of gaining peace at "the brink of war." The United States moved atomic missiles to Okinawa. Mr. Dulles told Prime Minister Nehru of India, who would pass the news to Peiping, that, unless a settlement were made along or near the thirty-eighth parallel, the United States would bomb beyond the Yalu River and would use "tactical" atomic arms if necessary. We cannot know whether these threats were useful. We do know that Stalin died on March 5 and that on March 28 the Communists agreed to the exchange of sick and injured prisoners. They added that they now wished to discuss "the smooth settlement of the entire question of prisoners of war." Thereafter, the limited victory was endangered far more by Syngman Rhee than by the Russians or the Chinese.

The major problem, aside from Syngman Rhee, was whether prisoners who did not choose to return to North Korea should be repatriated by force. President Eisenhower, with fifty-four members of the United Nations behind him, said "No." The Communists gave ground. By the middle of June a settlement seemed likely. But on the eighteenth of that month Mr. Rhee released twenty-seven thousand anti-Communist North Korean prisoners. These were the men about whom the argument raged, so the Communists had reason to be annoyed. Vociferously, they charged that the Americans had "connived" at the action. They demanded that the prisoners be recaptured—an unlikely task in those bleak hills. Yet the negotiations went forward. Clearly, if Mr. Rhee could be brought to his senses, the long-sought truce was at hand. The President sent an Assistant Secretary of State to argue with South Korea.

"Peace" and the Bandung Conference

Mr. Rhee could quote Senators Knowland and Taft—a truce on the thirty-eighth parallel was "extremely unsatisfactory." The South Korean troops, by this time, held two-thirds of the line. If Mr. Rhee ordered them to attack or if he simply pulled them out and sent them home, the small remaining forces of the United Nations would be in a poor plight. And Syngman Rhee was notable for stubbornness. Luckily, he made a graceful concession: he dissociated himself from the truce, but he would abide by it. He would give the United Nations a chance to unify Korea by political agreement. He did not promise to be docile if the United Nations failed; neither did he boast that he would go to war with Asia all by himself. The United States gave him one reassurance: the President would go "all out" if the North Koreans renewed the war after the truce. This, according to Admiral Radford, meant the "use of atomic weapons, if necessary."

On July 28, 1953, the truce was signed at Panmunjom. No South Korean name was attached. The "police action" had lasted for more than thirty-seven months. The American casualties were 33,629 dead and 103,284 wounded. The frontier was little changed from that of 1950. There were no forced repatriations. There was no system of inspection to insure that the Communists could not prepare for a new attack. The victory was "limited"—yet the North Korean aggression had not accomplished its purpose.

Although the terms were weaker than those he had himself

proposed, Mr. Truman asked the American people to support the President. The people responded. The President had his way in spite of grumblings from Republican senators. The last step was customary and taken for granted: Congress appropriated two hundred million dollars to begin rebuilding Korea.

2

Now that he had ended hostilities in Korea, the President's next job was to end them at home—to bring that absence of crossness that it is his genius to inspire. He could not make a proper start until the voters relieved him of the Republican Congress. The senators in his own party behaved cantankerously, as if they really believed the promises they had made during the campaign. Angry at the failure to enforce "victory" in Korea, they were still more angry at the failure to balance the budget and to reduce taxes.

For years they had scorned Mr. Truman's policy of "containment." It meant huge expenditures for armaments and foreign aid, it meant a careful concern for the prejudices of our allies, it meant admitting that the world-wide maladjustments could not be ignored. By temperament and by their self-indulgent dream that America could get what she wanted if she really tried, these senators believed in "going it alone." The President had seen the world and had no such illusions. But he tried, wisely, to placate his Senate. Mr. Dulles announced a new policy: "a maximum deterrent" at "a bear-

able cost." Hence the talk about "a great capacity to re-
taliate, instantly, by means and at times of our own choos-
ing"; hence the talk about "an agonizing reappraisal of basic
United States policy" if the French did not do what they were
told.

Tocqueville, on the whole, gave an agreeable account of
American democracy; yet he feared that it must perish in the
end because of the inexorable pressure of foreign policy.
"Foreign politics," he wrote, "demand scarcely any of those
qualities which are peculiar to a democracy; they require, on
the contrary, the perfect use of almost all those in which it is
deficient. . . . A democracy can only with great difficulty
regulate the details of an important undertaking, persevere in
a fixed design, and work out its execution in spite of serious
obstacles. It cannot combine its measures with secrecy or
await their consequences with patience." The Republican
Senate, which Mr. Eisenhower sought to lure gently toward
an adult understanding of life, might have been elected to
prove Tocqueville's point.

In part, as we have seen, this was an accident of history:
the Republicans had been out of power on each occasion when
America had been forced to learn the necessity of Europe.
Since it was their duty to prove that Democrats were wrong,
they made Asia their province and their special care. Then
Asia in the person of China turned savagely hostile, while
Asia in the person of India turned suspiciously and super-

ciliously neutral. So they were left with their natural American impatience—i.e., "go it alone."

The President soothed them by promising that he would be "positive" in dealing with Communist powers. He said he had not forgotten the campaign promises of "liberation." In fact, we could not be even mildly positive without the help of our great allies, and we could liberate nobody short of a world war. Step by step—protesting always that it was now very different, very Republican—the Administration found itself back with the policy of containment, with the policy of foreign aid, with the policy of dignified dealings toward our allies, and with the new burden of explaining always that Mr. Dulles had not meant what he seemed to be saying. (In most cases this was true. Mr. Dulles has a talent for expressing the mildest notion in a way to make it sound dangerous and annoying.)

This unadmitted return toward the policies of Mr. Truman and Mr. Acheson meant that taxes remained high and the budget remained unbalanced. The Administration made a workman-like and responsible attempt at economy, but the Congress remained surly. In November, 1954, however, the voters gave Mr. Eisenhower a new Congress: 49 Democratic senators to 47 Republicans; 230 Democrats in the House of Representatives and 201 Republicans. Slightly to the surprise of the nation and immensely to the surprise of the President, this was a good arrangement. The President's gentle leadership was well adapted to a form of coalition. The senior Democrats in both Houses were glad to prove their sense of responsibility.

In July, 1954, for the first time since the Japanese invasion of Manchuria, there was no acknowledged war anywhere. Peace had broken out, however briefly.[1] This may have helped to promote the new feeling in America—the feeling that doom was receding, that man might have a breathing-spell to reassess his problems and perhaps to come to terms with them. The chief source of this feeling was unquestionably Mr. Eisenhower. Less harassed than in the days of the Republican Congress, more at home amid the perplexing tasks of the presidency, he found his true place as a national, rather than as a party, leader.

All American Presidents have a dual role—head of the party and head of the nation. In a constitutional monarchy the prime minister is head of the party, and the head of the nation is the king. The President is both. After a slow start, General Eisenhower has become a politician in the high sense of the word. His party cannot do without him. And in his other role, as head of the nation, he is equally indispensable. He is the kindly, friendly man who reconciles difficulties rather than slashing through them. After the ten years of Yalta, Potsdam, Berlin, Hiss, Fuchs, Korea, McCarthy, and the bomb, the nation wanted such a man.

1. The price of this unaccustomed peace had been the "agreement" in Indochina.

The Price of Power

Tocqueville charged democracy with the vague misuse of moral terms when dealing with foreign affairs. A good example of this confusion is the emotion attached to the word "power," as in "power politics" and "balance of power." From childish days we think of power as something bad that must be restrained, just as big children are restrained from beating little children in the nursery. But power has no moral content; it merely exists to be used for good or evil, as an airplane exists to carry medicine or passengers or bombs.

"Power politics" is a redundancy, since politics cannot operate without power. When the farmers organize to seek favors at Washington or the labor unions or the watchmakers, we call it "pressure politics," hoping to distinguish it from power politics, because power is bad and is used by foreigners. Yet the wise application of power (or pressure) is the meaning of political science and the one hope for composing grievances, domestic or foreign. When politics end, war begins—unless the community contains a number of groups of roughly equal strength. In that case the unaggrieved majority will tend to draw together, in its own interest, to forbid an appeal to arms. But this balance cannot be maintained between two powers alone.

During the decades of turbulence before the American Civil War, the ever renewed West was a balance between the old North and the old South. Then the West, too, caught fire

172

and joined sides. Power became polarized between two centers; politics dissolved into revolution. During the first years
of the twentieth century, when the six strong nations of Europe divided into the Triple Alliance and the Triple Entente,
no balancing group remained, and the result was war.

The whole world was in a similar predicament during the
first years of the atomic age. The poles of power were Moscow and Washington. Because of the bomb, the remaining
four-fifths of the human race could not provide a balance, so
mankind teetered on the brink of death. But toward the end of
the decade signs of hope appeared. The Marshall Plan had
released western Europe from poverty and subservience. The
death of Stalin had encouraged a restive stirring among the
satellites of eastern Europe. Great Britain was on the verge of
applying atomic energy to industry. The bomb was no longer
the monopoly of Moscow and Washington. And the world-
continent of Asia-Africa took the first step at Bandung toward concerting a policy.

Ten years and six days after Roosevelt's death and Mr.
Truman's hurried inauguration, the Bandung conference met
in Indonesia. Twenty-nine nations were represented, but no
Western leader was present. More than half the population
of the world was represented, but the white man had no
spokesman. Here was the beginning of a new age and the end
of the age that had begun with the industrial revolution of the
eighteenth century.

The Price of Power

The first industrial revolution made the West incontinently stronger than the "backward" peoples—whether they were backward in the sense of a Central African savage or merely in the sense of lacking steam engines and rapid-fire weapons. Such a great and sudden disparity in transport and in fighting strength made all the rest of the planet into a power vacuum. It made no difference how many people lived in an area, how ancient their civilization, or how pure their religion; without steam and steel they were in a power vacuum just as certainly as Hungary was in a power vacuum when the armies of the West were disbanded in 1945. And just as Russian power flowed into Hungary, so did the power of the whole industrialized West flow into Asia and Africa. The great colonial age had begun. And with the Bandung conference the great colonial age came to an end.

"The voiceless ones," said President Soekarno of the Republic of Indonesia, had recovered their voices. "Man gasps for safety and morality," he added, "in a world of fear." He begged the conference: "Do not be guided by these fears, because fear is an acid which etches man's actions into curious patterns. Be guided by hopes and determination, be guided by ideals, and, yes, be guided by dreams!" And he called for the mobilization of "the moral violence of Nations" in favor of peace.

This would have been just another pretty speech, another cry from the heart of helpless people, except for the presence of China at the conference in the person of Chou En-lai. The Premier was constructive, conciliatory, clearly bent on promoting the maximum of unity among the recently "voiceless ones." And China, having become a nation, disposes of power: some power today, immense power in the future. She may call upon yesterday's colonies to redress the balance of tomorrow.

We are not suggesting that the age of colonialism was bad merely because we notice that it has come to an end. In the first place, it was inevitable, given the industrial revolution. And, in the second place, it did permanent good, whereas its harm is already passing away. The medicine, the technology, the engineering, the sanitation, the uncorrupted civil services of the West—these are useful contributions. And Christianity was a good thing to offer, whether people chose to listen or not. Perhaps if the wives of the civil servants, officers, and colonial administrators had been less rude, less delighted with the chance to pretend they were superior, the entire era might have left a better taste. But, whether or not we liked it while it lasted, the era is ended. Yesterday's "voiceless ones" no longer live in a power vacuum. Indeed, if the West continues the self-destruction on which it has been so busy since 1914—and if it does not accidentally poison the air for all mankind—Pittsburgh and Manchester may soon be the power vacuums.

The men of Bandung, representing the great land mass from

Japan to the heart of Africa, agreed on one thing: to steer clear, if possible, from the deadly quarrels of the West. The West has been oddly naïve about this decision. The American government, for example, has seemed at times to be surprised that India has chosen "neutralism" instead of gladly throwing in her lot with us. Yet the same government will explain to Mr. Nehru that if it is not offered an end to the stalemate in Korea it is prepared to use atomic weapons, which might mean the destruction not only of all Americans but of all Indians as well. Watching the West, with its inextinguishable hatreds and its illimitable ability to kill, the "neutral" people must yearn at times to move to another planet. Luckily for the rest of us, they cannot—at least for the next few years.

The delegates at the Bandung conference were frightened by the hostility between China and the United States. They felt that the whole of Asia was threatened, to say nothing of the whole of the human race. Chou En-lai, therefore, suggested a meeting between the Chinese and the Americans, in the hope of relaxing the tension. The talks were held at Geneva and led to nothing useful in the first instance; yet they may have helped us to think of the Chinese once again as people, not ogres, and as people whom we were proud to honor yesterday. The wounds and the insults of Korea still rankle, but, as the President has said, if we remember what we recently thought about the Germans and the Japanese, we should not regard our distaste for China as eternal.

"Peace" and the Bandung Conference

Mr. Eisenhower has never accepted the official Republican attitude toward China. Senators Jenner and Dirksen strove in 1953 to commit him to permanent enmity toward the government at Peiping. The Appropriations Committee of the Senate, by a vote of twenty to three, reported a bill that would cancel American contributions to the United Nations if Communist China were admitted. The President, for once, used his full influence, and the project was defeated.

Eighteen months after the conference at Bandung, Mr. Eisenhower was re-elected with an even greater majority than he had received in 1952, and with a Democratic Congress. Since the Democrats have been chiefly concerned with their own ocean, they have made relatively few silly speeches about the Pacific. The President has a free hand and an immense authority. He can easily persuade his fellow citizens to stop pretending that the five hundred million men and women of Communist China are waiting impatiently for the return of Chiang Kai-shek. In other words, the re-election of Mr. Eisenhower and of a Democratic Congress changed none of our problems and left us free to find the wisest solutions we are able to devise. Our best-loved citizen remains in the White House. The Congress will support him when he is bold and imaginative but may well grow restive and stubborn if he fails to supply the leadership which is the prerogative of his office and without which the United States cannot discharge the duties imposed upon her during these awe-inspiring years.

The Price of Power

4

The world today has grounds for a sober hope, in spite of the bomb and in spite of the recent martyrdom of Hungary. In Mazzini's phrase, "the inexorable logic of facts" demands that we appeal to a long-neglected form of power—the power of thought.

The intercontinental ballistic missile, we are told, will soon bring Russia and the United States within twenty-four minutes of each other. The human race will then be within twenty-four minutes of catastrophe should anyone in Moscow or Washington become overeager. "The world," says Ambassador Romulo of the Republic of the Philippines, "is a year or so away from a point of no return. . . . In a year or so we must have in operation a system of enforceable control over all devices for depopulation. If we do not, we shall soon enter an era of sleepless waiting for mounting 'mutual terror' to explode into mutual annihilation." And the Ambassador adds that it is irresponsible nonsense to assume that "mutual terror" can secure peace. A two-power world can never be at peace. Frightened men cannot be trusted to refrain from pushing that all-decisive button.

We now have the wherewithal to abolish mankind, so what larger terrors do we need? Why not admit that all things changed forever at Potsdam, when the news came that those "babies" had been "satisfactorily born"? At that moment, as we have said, war lost its immemorial meaning; so why not seek a substitute? Why not attempt new thoughts for our new world? If we truly believed and felt the danger, we would accept the adventure.

The imagination of half of mankind was released at Bandung. We shall meet with help as well as with competition if we seek to use the power of thought. But we shall not be heeded—we of the West—unless we lift our tired minds to originality and daring.

Bibliographical Note

A faithful bibliography covering ten years of our recent history would be longer than this book. A selective bibliography is merely another way of expressing one's own views. How fortunate was Milton, who had only to master six languages in order to read all the known literature of his day. How fortunate was Gibbon, a hundred years later, who could read everything available which dealt with the Roman Empire, West and East. Had I the industry and the erudition of these great men, I could not read half what I should have read in order to write this book. So the following brief suggestions for further study must be regarded as unreliable, doubly unreliable since even the best books—containing what might be called "source material"—cannot be taken too seriously because they cannot yet be weighed against the papers, letters, and reminiscences of other men with divergent views.

For example, the most rewarding book in my bibliography, for the years 1949–51, is *The Private Papers of Senator Vanderberg*. Yet one of the reasons for its pre-eminence is that the private papers of so many other important men have not yet been published. We cannot today balance the judgments of Arthur Vandenberg against those of his peers. So the reader must beware.

Bibliographical Note

THE AMERICAN SCENE, GENERAL

ALLEN, FREDERICK L. *The Big Change.* New York, 1952.

JOHNSON, GERALD W. *Incredible Tale: The Odyssey of the Average American in the Last Half Century.* New York, 1950.

JUNGK, ROBERT. *Tomorrow Is Already Here.* New York, 1954.

RIESMAN, DAVID, et al. *The Lonely Crowd.* New Haven, 1950.

VIERECK, PETER R. E. *The Shame and Glory of the Intellectuals.* Boston, 1953.

GOVERNMENT AND POLITICS

AGAR, HERBERT. *The Price of Union.* Boston, 1950.

BINKLEY, WILFRED E. *American Political Parties.* New York, 1943.

BROGAN, DENIS W. *Politics in America.* New York, 1954.

BROWN, JOHN M. *Through These Men.* New York, 1956.

CORWIN, EDWARD S. *The President: Office and Powers, 1787–1948.* 3d rev. ed. New York, 1948.

DANIELS, JONATHAN. *The Man from Independence.* Philadelphia, 1950.

DONOVAN, ROBERT J. *Eisenhower: The Inside Story.* New York, 1956.

GALBRAITH, JOHN K. *Economics and the Art of Controversy.* New Brunswick, N.J., 1955.

GOLDMAN, ERIC F. *The Crucial Decade.* New York, 1956.

KOENIG, LOUIS W. (ed.). *Truman Administration.* New York, 1956.

LARSON, ARTHUR. *A Republican Looks at His Party.* New York, 1956.

LUBELL, SAMUEL. *The Future of American Politics.* New York, 1952.

———. *The Revolt of the Moderates.* New York, 1956.

PUSEY, MERLO J. *Eisenhower the President.* New York, 1956.

ROVERE, RICHARD H. *Affairs of State: The Eisenhower Years.* New York, 1956.

SEVAREID, ERIC. *Small Sounds in the Night.* New York, 1956.

SHERWOOD, ROBERT E. *Roosevelt and Hopkins.* New York, 1948.

The Price of Power

Stevenson, Adlai E. *Call to Greatness*. New York, 1954.

———. *What I Think*. New York, 1956.

Truman, Harry S. *Year of Decisions*. New York, 1955.

———. *Years of Trial and Hope*. New York, 1956.

ECONOMICS

Berle, Adolph A. *The 20th Century Capitalist Revolution*. New York, 1954.

Fortune Editors. *U.S.A.: The Permanent Revolution*. New York, 1951.

———. *The Changing American Market*. New York, 1955.

Galbraith, John K. *American Capitalism*. Boston, 1952.

Lilienthal, David E. *Big Business: A New Era*. New York, 1953.

Millis, Harry A., and Brown, Emily C. *From the Wagner Act to Taft-Hartley*. Chicago, 1950.

THE ATOM AND MILITARY POLICY

Bradley, David V. *No Place To Hide*. Boston, 1948.

Bush, Vannevar. *Modern Arms and Free Men*. New York, 1949.

Dean, Gordon E. *Report on the Atom*. New York, 1953.

Lang, Daniel. *The Man in the Thick Lead Suit*. New York, 1954.

U.S. Congress, Joint Committee on Atomic Energy. *The Hydrogen Bomb and Its Control*. Washington, 1950 (81st Cong., 2d sess.).

U.S. Department of State. *International Control of Atomic Energy*. 3 vols. Washington, 1946–49.

SUBVERSION, SECURITY, THE THREAT TO CIVIL LIBERTIES

Andrews, Bert. *Washington Witch Hunt*. New York, 1948.

Barth, Alan. *Government by Investigation*. New York, 1955.

Chambers, Whittaker. *Witness*. New York, 1952.

Commager, Henry C. *Freedom, Loyalty, and Dissent*. New York, 1954.

Bibliographical Note

COOKE, ALISTAIR. *A Generation on Trial*. New York, 1950.

CORWIN, EDWARD S. *Total War and the Constitution*. New York, 1947.

DAVIS, ELMER H. *But We Were Born Free*. Indianapolis, 1954.

ERNST, MORRIS L., and LOTH, DAVID. *Report on the American Communist*. New York, 1952.

HAND, LEARNED. *The Spirit of Liberty*. New York, 1952.

HICKS, GRANVILLE. *Where We Came Out*. New York, 1954.

JOWITT, WILLIAM A. J. *The Strange Case of Alger Hiss*. Garden City, 1953.

LATTIMORE, OWEN. *Ordeal by Slander*. Boston, 1950.

PHILBRICK, HERBERT A. *I Led Three Lives*. New York, 1952.

WECHSLER, JAMES A. *The Age of Suspicion*. New York, 1953.

WISCONSIN CITIZENS COMMITTEE. *The McCarthy Record*. Madison, 1952.

EDUCATION

CONANT, JAMES B. *Education in a Divided World*. Cambridge, 1948.

CURTI, MERLE E. (ed.). *American Scholarship in the Twentieth Century*. Cambridge, 1953.

GINZBURG, ELI, and BRAY, DOUGLAS W. *The Uneducated*. New York, 1953.

MACIVER, ROBERT M. *Academic Freedom in Our Time*. New York, 1955.

FOREIGN RELATIONS

ACHESON, DEAN G. *A Democrat Looks at His Party*. New York, 1955.

BEMIS, SAMUEL F. *The U.S. as a World Power: A Dipolmatic History, 1900–1950*. New York, 1950.

COUNCIL ON FOREIGN RELATIONS. *The U.S. in World Affairs, 1945–1947*. New York, 1947 (and annually thereafter).

DAVIS, ELMER H. *Two Minutes to Midnight*. Indianapolis, 1955.

DULLES, FOSTER R. *America's Rise to World Power, 1898–1954*. New York, 1954.

The Price of Power

FINLETTER, THOMAS K. *Power and Policy*. New York, 1954.

KENNAN, GEORGE F. *American Diplomacy, 1900–1950*. Chicago, 1951.

———. *Realities of American Foreign Policy*. Princeton, 1954.

LUBELL, SAMUEL. *The Revolution in World Trade and American Economic Policy*. New York, 1955.

ROBERTS, HENRY L. *Russia and America: Dangers and Prospects*. New York, 1956.

TAFT, ROBERT A. *A Foreign Policy for Americans*. New York, 1951.

THORP, WILLARD L. *Trade, Aid, or What?* Baltimore, 1954.

VANDENBERG, ARTHUR J., JR., AND MORRIS, J. A. *The Private Papers of Senator Vandenberg*. Boston, 1952.

WOODROW WILSON FOUNDATION. *U.S. Foreign Policy*. New York, 1953.

———. *The Political Economy of American Foreign Policy*. New York, 1955.

FOREIGN RELATIONS, FAR EAST

CLARK, MARK. *From the Danube to the Yalu*. New York, 1954.

FEIS, HERBERT. *The China Tangle*. Princeton, 1953.

GUNTHER, JOHN. *The Riddle of MacArthur*. New York, 1951.

POATS, RUTHERFORD M. *Decision in Korea*. New York, 1954.

ROVERE, RICHARD H., AND SCHLESINGER, ARTHUR M. *The General and the President*. New York, 1951.

U.S. DEPARTMENT OF STATE. *U.S. Relations with China, with Special Reference to the Period 1944–1949*. Washington, 1949.

Important Dates

Yalta Conference, February 4–11

U.S. forces invade Iwo Jima, February 19

U.S. forces invade Okinawa, April 1

President Roosevelt dies, Truman succeeds to the Presidency, April 12

Opening of San Francisco conference to organize United Nations, April 25

Germany surrenders, V-E Day, May 8

Churchill warns Truman of "iron curtain," May 12

Truman ignores Churchill warning, orders U.S. troops to withdraw into occupation zone, June 21

United Nations Charter signed, June 26

First atomic bomb tested at Alamogordo, New Mexico, July 16

Potsdam Conference, July 17–August 2

Attlee succeeds Churchill as Prime Minister, July 26

Senate ratifies United Nations Charter 89 to 2, July 28

A-bomb dropped on Hiroshima, August 6

Russia declares war on Japan, August 8

A-bomb dropped on Nagasaki, August 9

Japan surrenders, V-J Day, August 14

Foreign ministers meet in London to draft peace treaties with Italy and Nazi satellites, September

Truman, Attlee, and King agree that A-bomb secrets will not be shared until the United Nations devises firm control plan, November 15

Second foreign ministers' conference on peace treaties in Moscow, December

1946   Churchill's "iron curtain" address at Fulton, Missouri, March 5

Third foreign ministers' conference on peace treaties in Paris, April

Truman seizes railroads to avert strike, May 17

Truman asks Congress to authorize draft of striking railroad workers; strike settled, May 24

U.S. plan for control of atomic energy presented to United Nations, June 14

Atomic tests at Bikini, July 1

McMahon bill signed, establishing Atomic Energy Commission, August 1

Wallace speech opposing U.S. policy toward Russia, September 12

Wallace fired from Cabinet, September 20

Republicans win both Houses of Congress, November 5

1947   Iran charges in United Nations that Russia interferes in her internal affairs, January 19

Marshall succeeds Byrnes as Secretary of State, January 21

Russia rejects U.S. plan for control of atomic energy, March 4

Important Dates

Truman announces Truman Doctrine, asks Congress for funds, May 12

Congress authorizes appropriation for Truman Doctrine, May 15

Reds take over Hungary, April 30

Marshall enunciates Marshall Plan at Harvard, June 5

Taft-Hartley Act becomes law over Truman's veto, June 23

Moscow announces formation of new Cominform, October 5

1948   Reds take over Czechoslovakia, February 25

Benelux nations, England, and France sign fifty-year alliance, March 17

Congress passes Marshall Plan, April 2

Truman signs Marshall Plan bill, April 3

Russia blockades Berlin, June 19

Berlin airlift begins, June 21

Thomas Dewey wins Republican nomination, June 24

Truman wins Democratic nomination, July 15

Truman orders integration of Negroes in armed forces, July 26

Republic of Korea proclaimed, August 15

Whittaker Chambers charges Alger Hiss with Communist membership, August 17

Truman re-elected, Democrats win both Houses of Congress, November 2

Chambers accuses Hiss of espionage, December 6

Hiss indicted for perjury, December 15

1949   Acheson succeeds Marshall as Secretary of State, January 18

Berlin blockade and airlift ends, May 12

Senate ratifies NATO, July 21

The Price of Power

State Department issues White Paper on China explaining loss to Communists, August 5

Chinese Communists proclaim Peoples Republic, September 21

Truman announces that Russia has the A-bomb, September 23

Chinese Nationalist government flees to Formosa, December

1950   Acheson address excluding Korea from U.S. defense perimeter, January 12

Hiss convicted, January 21

Truman orders Atomic Energy Commission to develop H-bomb, January 31

Britain announces confession of Fuchs as atom spy, February 3

Senator McCarthy address at Wheeling, West Virginia, charging Communists in State Department, February 9

Congressional inquiry into "5 per centers" and Reconstruction Finance Corporation, January, February

Supreme Court bars segregation in colleges and railroad cars, June 5

Republic of Korea invaded by North Korean Communists, June 24

United Nations orders North Koreans to withdraw, June 25

Truman orders U.S. sea and air forces to aid Republic of Korea, orders Seventh Fleet to Formosa, June 26

United Nations Security Council calls on all members to aid in resisting North Korean aggression, June 27

Seoul falls to North Koreans, June 29

Truman orders U.S. ground forces into conflict on recommendation of General MacArthur, June 30

MacArthur named United Nations commander, July 8

Important Dates

United Nations forces land at Inchon, open counteroffen-
sive, September 15
Liberation of Seoul completed, September 28
President Rhee returns to Seoul, September 29
United Nations adopts resolution to unify Korea, authorizes
operations north of thirty-eighth parallel, October 7
Truman and MacArthur confer at Wake Island, October 15
Democrats hold both Houses of Congress in election, No-
vember 7
U.S. troops reach Manchurian border, November 20

1951 Twenty-second Amendment to Constitution adopted, limit-
ing President to two terms, February 26
MacArthur intimates attack on China, offers to confer on
terms, March 24
Truman recalls MacArthur, April 11
MacArthur addresses Congress, "Old Soldier" speech,
April 19
Congressional committee hearings on MacArthur recall,
May 9—June 5
Senator McCarthy attacks General Marshall as part of
Communist conspiracy, June 14
Russia proposes truce in Korea, June 23
Truce talks begin in Korea, July 10
Churchill returns as Prime Minister, November 8

1952 Truman seizes steel mills to avert strike, April 8
West Germany and Allies sign peace contract, May 26
Supreme Court rules Truman's seizure of steel mills illegal,
June 2
Eisenhower wins Republican nomination, July 11
Stevenson wins Democratic nomination, July 26

The Price of Power

Eisenhower elected President, Republicans take both Houses of Congress, November 4

Atomic Energy Commission announces successful H-bomb tests at Eniwetok, November 10

1953 McCarthy attacks U.S. Information Service, February 17
Stalin dies, March 5
Malenkov named Premier of U.S.S.R., March 6
Chinese Communists offer to exchange prisoners in Korea and settle entire prisoner-of-war question, March 28
Agreement reached on prisoner-of-war question at Panmunjom, June 8
East Berlin uprising against Communists, June 17
President Rhee releases Chinese and North Korean prisoners, June 18
Korean Armistice signed, July 28
Taft dies, July 31
Russia announces possession of H-bomb, August 20

1954 Dulles enunciates doctrine of "massive retaliation," January 12
McCarthy attacks General Zwicker in course of hearings on Communists in Army, February 18
Army charges McCarthy sought preferential treatment for Schine, March 11
Congress holds Army-McCarthy hearings, April 22—June 17
Supreme Court bans segregation in public schools, May 17
Indochina truce signed at Geneva, giving half of Viet-Nam to Communists, July 21
Watkins committee recommends Senate censure McCarthy, September 27
Agreement signed granting West Germany sovereignty, permitting her to rearm and join NATO, October 23

Important Dates

Democrats regain both Houses of Congress, November 2

Senate censures McCarthy, December 2

1955 Eisenhower asks Congress for authority to defend Formosa
      and Pescadores against Chinese Communist attack, Janu-
      ary 24

      Congress approves, January 28

      Bulganin succeeds Malenkov as Premier of U.S.S.R., Feb-
      ruary 8

      Churchill resigns as Prime Minister, April 5

      Eden succeeds him, April 6

      Bandung Conference, April 18–27

      "Summit Conference" at Geneva, July 18–23

      Eisenhower suffers heart attack, September 24

1956 Khrushchev denounces Stalin, February 24

      Eisenhower announces intention to seek second term, Feb-
      ruary 29

      Cominform dissolved, April 17

      Eisenhower stricken with ileitis, June 8

      British occupation of Suez ends, June 13

      U.S. withdraws pledge to help Egypt build Aswan Dam,
      July 19

      Egypt seizes Suez Canal, July 26

      Stevenson wins Democratic nomination, August 16

      Eisenhower renominated, August 22

      Poland successfully asserts partial independence of Moscow,
      October 19

      Soviet forces begin to crush Hungarian uprising, October 24

      Israel invades Egypt, October 29

      England and France invade Egypt, October 31

      Eisenhower re-elected, Democrats win both Houses of Con-
      gress, November 6

Index

Index

Index

missed by Truman, 131, 134–35, 189 (date); "fades away," 135–38, 189 (date); intimates attack on China, offers to confer, 130–31, 189 (date); in Korean War, 124–31; on need for Soviet participation in war against Japan, 34; quarrels with Truman, 129–31

McCarthy, Joseph Raymond, 5, 105, 106–15, 146, 160; adverse effects of, on U.S. prestige abroad, 153–54; attacks Army, 155; attacks General Marshall, 138, 140, 145, 155, 189 (date); attacks General Zwicker, 156, 190 (date); attacks U.S. Information Service, 152–54, 190 (date); breaks with Eisenhower, 158; censured by Senate, 158; censured by Senate Committee on Rules and Administration, 115; characterized, 155; on Communists in State Department, 108–9; compared to Huey Long, 111; decline and fall of, 158–59; Denver speech of, 109; early career of, 106; Eisenhower's weakness before, 153; at height of power, 112; judged worst Senator by American Political Science Association, 112; press and, 112–13; Senate complaisance regarding, 110–11, 115; success of, reasons for, 109–11, 113–14; in Tydings election, role of, 114–16; Wheeling speech of, 107–9, 188 (date)

McCormick, Robert R., 104

Machiavelli, Niccolò, 20, 21

Malenkov, Georgi M., 190, 191

Malmédy massacre, 107

Malone, George W., 165

Manchuria, 34, 35, 36, 97, 127, 137, 171

Mao Tse-tung, 97, 98

Marshall, George C., 14, 34, 76; attacked by McCarthy, 138, 140, 145, 155, 189 (date); becomes Secretary of State, 70, 186 (date);

Harvard speech announcing Marshall Plan, 74, 187 (date)

Marshall Plan, 6, 69, 72–79, 107; effects of, 173; passed by Congress, 78, 187 (dates)

Martin, Joseph W., 134

Mazzini, Giuseppe, 178

Middle East, 70, 101

Military influence on postwar situation, 37–39

Molotov, Vyacheslav M., 13–15; at Paris meeting of Council of Foreign Ministers, 52; at San Francisco conference, 15

Mongolia, outer, 36

Moscow conference, 186 (date)

Mutual Security Program, 160

National Lawyers Guild, 157

Negroes in U.S., 141; and foreign policy, 7; integration of, in armed forces, ordered by Truman, 132, 187 (date); and Korean War, 132–33; segregation of, in schools, banned by Supreme Court, 190 (date)

Nehru, Jawaharlal, 7, 165, 176

Neisse, 33

New York Herald-Tribune, 113, 159

New York Times, 112

New York Times Book Review, 27

New Yorker, 123

Nixon, Richard Milhous, 96

North Atlantic Treaty Organization (NATO), 24, 69, 107–8

Oder-Neisse line, 31

Okinawa, 35, 165, 185

Open Door in China, 100

Oppenheimer, J. Robert, 8, 56

Pacific Ocean, 102

Panama Canal, 45

Panmunjom, 167, 190

Paris Conference of Foreign Ministers, 51–52, 186 (date)

Pearl Harbor, 98

Philbrick, Herbert, 113

Index

THE CHICAGO HISTORY OF AMERICAN CIVILIZATION

DANIEL J. BOORSTIN, *Editor*

EDMUND S. MORGAN
The Birth of the Republic: 1763–89

HOWARD H. PECKHAM
The War for Independence: A Military History

SAMUEL P. HAYS
The Response to Industrialism: 1885–1914

WILLIAM E. LEUCHTENBURG
The Perils of Prosperity: 1914–32

DEXTER PERKINS
The New Age of Franklin Roosevelt: 1932–45

HERBERT AGAR
The Price of Power: America since 1945

*   *

JOHN TRACY ELLIS
American Catholicism

NATHAN GLAZER
American Judaism